Dyslexia

Assessing and Reporting

The Patoss guide

Anwen Jones and Katherine Kindersley

in association with

THE PROFESSIONAL ASSOCIATION
OF TEACHERS OF STUDENTS WITH
SPECIFIC LEARNING DIFFICULTIES

HODDER
EDUCATION
AN HACHETTE UK COMPANY

Acknowledgements

We are greatly indebted to the editors of the first edition of this Patoss Guide to Assessing and Reporting. Gill Backhouse and Kath Morris have generously allowed us to use their work as a basis for this edition, but encouraged us to make substantial revisions to reflect all the change in the field. Similarly, the contributing authors to the first edition kindly released their work to Patoss, but their influence on this text remains considerable. Our thanks go to: Margaret Bevan, Valerie Hammond, Sue Kime, Bernadette McLean, Anne Mitchell, Nick Peacey, Prue Ruback, Liz Waine, Jennifer Watson and Annie White. The original text represented a significant step forward in guidance for specialist teachers and much has been retained.

In regard to this second edition, we would particularly like to acknowledge the encouragement and support of Lynn Greenwold, Chief Executive of Patoss, who has provided an overarching view throughout. Also, a dedicated group of colleagues have read a number of individual sections or chapters and shared their experience. Our very sincere thanks go to them all.

Although every effort has been made to ensure that website addresses are correct at time of going to press, Hodder Education cannot be held responsible for the content of any website referenced here. It is sometimes possible to find a relocated web page by typing in the address of the home page for a website in the URL window of your browser.

Hachette UK's policy is to use papers that are natural, renewable and recyclable products and made from wood grown in sustainable forests. The logging and manufacturing processes are expected to conform to the environmental regulations of the country of origin.

Orders: please contact Bookpoint Ltd, 130 Milton Park, Abingdon, Oxon OX14 4SB. Telephone: (44) 01235 827827. Fax: (44) 01235 400454. Lines are open 9.00–5.00, Monday to Saturday, with a 24-hour message answering service. Visit our website at www.hoddereducation.co.uk

First published 2013 by Hodder Education, part of Hachette UK, 338 Euston Road, London NW1 3BH

Copyright © 2013 Anwen Jones, Katherine Kindersley and Patoss
Cover photo © Abstractus Designus – Fotolia

Impression number 10 9 8 7 6 5 4 3 2 1
Year   2017 2016 2015 2014 2013

Typeset in New Century Schoolbook 10.5/14

Printed in Great Britain for Hodder Education, part of Hachette UK, 338 Euston Road, London NW1 3BH, by CPI Group (UK) Ltd, Croydon, CR0 4YY

A catalogue record for this title is available from the British Library.

ISBN 978 1 444 19034 2

Contents

Introduction   **vii**

What is Assessment? Why Assess?   **ix**

PART ONE Purpose, Principles and Practice   **1**

1. **Principles of Assessment**   **3**
The normal development of literacy skills. Dyslexia – definitions and
descriptions. Other SpLDs, co-occurrence and labelling.

2. **Basic Concepts in Psychometrics**   **25**
The normal distribution. Choosing the right tests. Using tests and test scores.
Describing scores. Comparing scores.

3. **Professional Practice**   **41**

PART TWO: Conducting the Assessment   **45**

4. **Practical Aspects of Assessment**   **47**
Prior checks. Screening. Assessment planning. The assessment session.

5. **Main Areas of Investigation**   **53**
Background Information. Cognitive Abilities. Attainments. Further
assessment areas. English as an additional language.

6. **Interpreting the Evidence: scores, observations and comparisons**   **69**
Verbal abilities. Non-verbal abilities. Verbal short-term and working memory.
Phonological awareness. Phonological processing speed. Visual processing
speed. Literacy. Reading. Spelling. Free writing. Numeracy. English as an
additional language. Synchronising the evidence. Perspectives on assessment
profiles.

7. **Assessment Profiles – Making Diagnostic Decisions**   **87**
Dyslexia. Dyspraxia. Dyscalculia. Specific language impairment. Attention
deficit hyperactivity disorder. Complicating factors.

8. **Recommendations and Working with Others**   **95**
    Working with other professionals. Collaboration and feedback.

9. **Writing the Assessment Report**   **103**
    General principles of report writing. The report structure and format. The
    main body of the report. Summaries and conclusions.

PART THREE: Through the Age Range   **115**

10. **The Early Years**   **117**
    Particular considerations for assessment in the early years. Early indicators
    of 'at risk' characteristics. Speech, language and vocabulary. Phonological
    abilities. Verbal short-term and working memory. Alphabet knowledge,
    reading and writing. Attention and perseverance. Motor coordination.
    Reaching conclusions.

11. **The Primary Phase**   **125**
    Particular considerations for the primary age range. Assessment at primary
    level. Intervention and recommendations. Outcomes of assessment: two case
    studies.

12. **The Secondary Phase**   **137**
    The transition to secondary school. Indicators of difficulty. Purposes
    of assessment. Assessment at secondary level. Report format and
    recommendations.

13. **Further Education**   **149**
    The FE environment – particular considerations. Screening in FE. Individual
    assessment in FE. Feedback and report format.

14. **Higher Education**   **159**
    Working within the HE sector. Reasons for referral and indicators of
    difficulty at HE level. Screening. The assessment. Recommendations and
    intervention at HE level.

PART FOUR: Resources and Reference   **171**

Miscue Analysis   173

Screening: An Alternative   175

Key Features of a Teaching Programme   178

Test Information   179

Test References   189

The authors

Anwen Jones is the SpLD Specialist in the Disability Advisory Service at the University of Oxford. She is a past Programme Director of Patoss, an experienced speaker at professional development events, and former course leader of the OCR qualifications in specialist SpLD teaching and assessment. Anwen is the current editor of *Dyslexia: Assessing the Need for Access Arrangements in Examinations* (2011) and she continues to assess and teach individuals with SpLD.

Katherine Kindersley is the founder Director of Dyslexia Assessment and Consultancy, a leading provider of assessment services for the workplace and secondary, further and higher education. She is a member of the Board of Directors of Patoss and is an experienced leader of a wide range of CPD events. Katherine was a contributing author to the first edition of this book and to *Dyslexia in the Workplace: An introductory guide* (2010). She is experienced in legal work and is a qualified expert witness.

The Professional Association of Teachers of Students with Specific Learning Difficulties (Patoss) works with the Joint Council for Qualifications, The Dyslexia-SpLD Trust, and the Department for Education, among other bodies, to promote good practice in assessing and teaching learners with difficulties. Patoss is especially active in recommending appropriate training, tests and report formats for a wide variety of purposes, including Disabled Students' Allowance and access arrangements in examinations, to SpLD/dyslexia assessors.

www.patoss-dyslexia.org

Acronyms

ADHD	Attention Deficit Hyperactivity Disorder
ALS	Additional Learning Support
APC	Assessment Practising Certificate
CPD	Continuing Professional Development
DBS	Disclosure Baring Service
DCD	Developmental Coordination Disorder
DCSF	Department for Children, Schools and Families
DfE	Department for Education
DfES	Department for Education and Skills
DSA	Disabled Students' Allowance
EYFS	Early Years Foundation Stage
FE	Further Education
GCE A-level	General Certificate of Education Advanced level
GCSE	General Certificate of Secondary Education
HCPC	Health and Care Professions Council
HE	Higher Education
IEP/ILP	Individual Education/Learning Plan
JCQ	Joint Council for Qualifications
LDD	Learning Difficulties and Disabilities
NICE	National Institute for Health and Care Excellence
Patoss	Professional Association of Teachers of Students with SpLD
SASC	SpLD Assessment Standards Committee
SD	Standard Deviation
SEN	Special Educational Need
SENCO	Special Educational Needs Coordinator
SEm	Standard Error of Measurement
SpLD/SpLDs	Specific Learning Difficulty/Difficulties
SLI	Specific Language Impairment

Introduction

Diagnostic assessment, where no two cases are alike, is demanding, intriguing and rewarding. It brings with it substantial professional responsibility, and decisions are not always easy. It is, however, also a privilege to work with individuals to change their lives for the better. A positive and professional assessment, which seeks strengths as well as weaknesses, conducted thoroughly and carefully with clear practical outcomes, can provide an entirely new way forward for an individual and this is what makes our task worthwhile.

This second edition of 'Assessing and Reporting' is a guide to current best practice in diagnostic assessment. Since publication of the first edition there has been significant change in the world of specific learning difficulties, and specialist teachers now play an increasingly important role in supporting children, young people and adults across many different settings. Developments in research, professional practice and government policy mean the context for assessment is always evolving.

Research continues to ask challenging questions and there is a growing focus on understanding the complexity and co-occurrence of specific learning difficulties. We reflect on these important theoretical issues here, although it proved impossible to cover everything. There will be many points where further research on the topics presented will be worthwhile and fascinating, and we hope this text inspires assessors to follow that path. We are all aware that we need to keep abreast of new knowledge as it emerges, so that our work is grounded firmly in well-established theory. There is also growing awareness of the social model of disability, encouraging recognition of the impact of external contextual factors on individuals at every level, whether in the classroom or the workplace, and this is to be welcomed.

The landscape of professional practice has also changed substantially in recent years. A new national standards body, the SpLD Assessment Standards Committee, is established and the Dyslexia-SpLD Trust is positioned to promote best practice and communication between all those interested in this field. Significant change is also brought about by developments in government policy and legislation, which means assessors find they must often respond to new circumstances.

It is against this background that this text has been substantially revised. In this new edition, Parts One and Two address the knowledge and skills needed by *all* assessors, regardless of the context in which they work. Part One addresses underpinning theory and is clearly applicable to all, but as assessment practice is also increasingly harmonised across the age ranges, the core knowledge – of how to conduct assessments, the main areas to investigate, interpretations to be made from the evidence and how to present reports – is brought together in Part Two. Having reviewed these sections, readers might turn to Part Three, which gives additional consideration to practice in each sector of education.

Given that change is the rule rather than the exception in the availability of test resources, we have elected not to recommend particular materials in the main text. New materials are published and old tests are put aside quite frequently, therefore a key skill of an assessor is the ability to evaluate the available tools. Readers can, however, turn to Part Four to see a list of some current resources, organised thematically for ease of reference.

Please note that to ease readability, the person assessed is referred to as 'he' while the assessor is referred to as 'she' throughout. Knowledge of the most common acronyms in our field is assumed and they are used generally without further expansion, but a list is provided for reference here.

Anwen Jones and Katherine Kindersley

What is assessment? Why assess?

Assessment is like an exploration, where we are unsure of the outcome and there is every possibility of discovering something new, or a detective story where we search for evidence to uncover more of the truth, or even a jigsaw puzzle where pieces are fitted together to create a picture. All of these are useful analogies, but they cast the person being assessed in a passive role; in contrast, we would like to stress the collaborative nature of assessment.

The child, young person or adult is actively involved at every stage and assessors work closely with fellow professionals, parents, carers, and possibly employers; many organisations and agencies might be involved. Clearly, therefore, assessment is not an isolated event, but part of an interactive process where people work together to understand an individual more fully and to promote his best interests.

'**Why assess?**' is a question which demands our attention and we should only begin an assessment when we have a clear view of the motivation for it – this will drive its focus and influence the tests chosen and the approach taken.

An assessment will commonly address concerns relating to educational progress. In the primary years, parents and teachers might notice children who are not achieving as expected and request an assessment. Later, at secondary school or college, new demands can present substantial challenges and questions are asked about whether specific difficulties might be at their root. Older students might seek an assessment to explore and explain difficulties they have faced in the past, perhaps after many years of frustration and misunderstanding.

An assessment might also be requested to meet legal obligations under the Equality Act, or to provide evidence of disability. At any age, having a formal diagnosis and a recognised name or label can provide a way to explain difficulties to others and open routes to funding for support. Other assessments might explore the need for access arrangements in examinations.

In every case, clear plans for intervention or adjustments must emerge – it is no use identifying a problem without suggesting a remedy – and recommendations to promote a dyslexia-friendly environment can go alongside personalised strategies and support.

Fundamentally, effective assessment is about facilitating change. It will empower the individual to use his strengths and understand his weaknesses, and give practical new strategies to support him in working towards his goals. Therefore, what is needed at the beginning of the assessment process is a clear view of what we hope to achieve at the end. The rest of this book is devoted to the journey in between.

PART ONE

Purpose, Principles and Practice

1 Principles of Assessment

The skill of an assessor extends far beyond knowing which tests to use and the methods necessary to calculate results – important as these are. For the competent professional, knowledge of the normal development of literacy skills and the relevant underlying cognitive processes, alongside the ability to recognise the signs of specific difficulties, analyse potential environmental influences and reflect on the impact of educational experience, are all essential pre-requisites. In this chapter we aim to give an overview of the key knowledge that informs diagnostic decisions, although all these skills will be developed throughout an assessment career and be strengthened by practical experience. We separate it into three sections.

- The normal development of literacy skills
- Dyslexia – definitions and descriptions – including discussion of a developmental model of SpLDs and features of the cognitive profile: phonological abilities, working memory and processing speed
- Other SpLDs – including dyspraxia, dyscalculia, ADHD and specific language impairment – and issues of co-occurrence and labelling

The normal development of literacy skills

Before we can begin any exploration of *difficulties* in literacy, a firm grasp of what is expected in *normal* development is needed. Children learn to speak long before they learn to read and write, and literacy is in effect 'spoken language in code'. To use spoken language effectively we must:

- know which sounds (phonemes), in which order, make a particular word (phonology);
- produce the word (articulation);
- know what words/phrases mean (semantics);
- know about grammar: word structure (morphology) and sentence structure (syntax);
- be able to use language to communicate with others (pragmatics).

In all these respects, spoken communication involves both listening *(reception)* and speaking *(expression)* and difficulties at any level will be reflected in the acquisition and use of literacy skills. This is because in English we convert speech into written language using an alphabetic code. The first task for beginners is to learn this code. We use 44 sounds – 20 vowel and 24 consonant sounds – and the task of mapping 26 abstract shapes which form the letters of the alphabet onto these sounds is a huge one. Signs of dyslexia often first become apparent when children have inordinate difficulty in 'cracking the code', using sounds to build basic word-level skills. The task is difficult not only for young minds, but it remains continually challenging as spoken vocabulary and the use of different grammatical constructions expands.

This process is further complicated as English is an extremely opaque language – the relationship between speech sounds and spelling patterns is not reliable. There is only one rule that really works – there must be at least one vowel, or a 'y', in every syllable – but we have a great many irregular words (*said, yacht*) and words where context must be relied on to work out meaning (homophones such as *there/their/they're* or *bean/been*). There is no doubt that becoming a proficient reader and speller in English is much harder than in more transparent languages such as Italian or Greek, where mapping letters onto speech sounds is a more straightforward affair.

The development of phonological awareness

The ability to identify, segment, blend and manipulate the sounds of spoken language is known as **phonological awareness**. It is not about hearing acuity but the efficient *processing* of sound information in the brain. When learning to read and spell, we need to analyse – or segment – words according to their sounds. Research has shown there is a common developmental pattern associated with this segmentation skill. Very young children are only able to identify fairly large 'chunks' of sound *(syllables)*, but they gradually become more discerning as awareness of alliteration and rhyme develop. Initially words are sub-divided into onsets and rimes, before more complex syllable structures are mastered. (The *onset* is the first consonant or consonant cluster in a word and the *rime* is what remains. For example, in *bread*, *'br'* is the onset and *'ead'* is the rime.) Eventually children learn to identify smaller units of sounds – phonemes – including consonant blends. Unstressed sounds such as /m/ and /n/ in final blends (*-mp, -nd*) are generally the last to be differentiated.

In the early years at school, children's phonological awareness develops as letter sounds are taught and they develop greater knowledge of sound-symbol correspondences *(phonics)*. When using phonics to read a word, they need to identify symbols, match them to sounds, blend the sounds together and then check whether they know such a word *(lexical checking)*. When spelling, they need to identify the sounds in words and then apply their knowledge of spelling patterns (*orthography* – the 'look' of a written word) to select the right letters. As children see patterns emerge, they can begin to read and spell.

Before we can judge whether a learner's skills are age-appropriate, or mildly delayed but following a normal pattern, or showing unusual signs as well as being delayed, we need to have a good grasp of what a normal development process looks like. Frith (1985)[1] sets out a model of the development of word-level reading and spelling skills which remains a useful starting point for everyday assessment, although it has been debated and developed by researchers subsequently.[2]

---

[1] Frith, U. (1985) *'Beneath the Surface of Developmental Dyslexia'*, in Patterson, K., Coltheart, M. and Marshall, J. (Eds) *Surface Dyslexia*, Routledge and Kegan Paul.

[2] For a useful review, see: Snowling, M.J. and Hulme, C. (Eds) (2007) *The Science of Reading: A Handbook* Blackwell.

This model describes a three-stage process (Figure 1.1):

1. *1.* The logographic stage is conceptualised as a visual strategy. Reading is accomplished through a 'look and guess' approach based on partial visual cues. It is inaccurate, and similar-looking words are muddled (e.g. sleep/steep/ sheep). The child has no decoding skills, so cannot work out unfamiliar words, and no encoding skills, so cannot spell accurately.

2. *2.* The alphabetic stage is where skills develop as sound-symbol knowledge grows and the child begins to 'crack the code'. In addition to reading some words by sight, he can now use sound-based strategies to decode and encode, therefore reading of unfamiliar words and spelling become possible. Emergent spelling requires considerable phonological awareness, as well as knowledge of sound-symbol correspondence.

3. *3.* The orthographic stage is where this knowledge is consolidated. The reader is now in a position to combine visual clues and sound-based (phonic) strategies to read and spell. As reading experience and spelling instruction become integrated with semantic and grammatical knowledge, much word-specific 'sub-lexical' knowledge (applying to divisions within words) is also acquired. Spelling rules, common spelling patterns (e.g. /-tion/, /-een/, /-ed/, /-ing/, irregular forms, homophones, etc) are mastered. Research has shown that morphological processing skills have an independent role to play in reading, in addition to phonological processing. (A morpheme is the smallest unit in a word that carries meaning – for example, *unreadable* has three morphemes: *un-read-able*.)

	Reading	**Spelling**
Logographic stage	Early reading is *BY SIGHT*. Reliance is on visual strategies. Learning is by 'Look and say'. New words cannot be read. Similar looking words are muddled.	Spelling is not yet possible.
Alphabetic stage	Ability to work out new words using phonics develops. Sight vocabulary and accuracy increases.	Early spelling is *BY SOUND*. Spelling is phonetic – i.e. it sounds right. (Awareness of sounds in speech *AND* sound-symbol correspondence are necessary pre-skills.)
Orthographic stage	Fluent, accurate reading depends on an amalgamation of visual and phonic strategies. Attention is paid to both the overall shape and the internal structure of a word.	Correct spelling develops as a result of spelling instruction *AND* reading experience, semantic and syntactic knowledge. Additional attention is given to visual as well as sound patterns – i.e. does it 'look right'?

Figure 1.1

It should be emphasised that these 'stages' are not discrete phases that children move into at particular ages. Rather, they form part of an ongoing and gradual process as the relevant strategies develop and word-specific knowledge is acquired.

A useful aspect of this model is that it offers an explanation of why children can often read words they cannot spell, and write words they cannot read. The hypothesis is that, in the early stages, they use different strategies for the two tasks: reading by sight, but spelling by sound. Then gradually the two processes start to interact, one feeding into the other in a dynamic way. It follows, therefore, that early spelling ability will be a better predictor of reading progress than early 'logographic' reading success.

The model offers a method of evaluating word-level reading and spelling to see if they appear 'acceptable' from a developmental perspective. Initially, young children may well only use a few letters to represent the dominant sounds in a word (e.g. *lk* for *look*) but they are presented in the correct order. Later, words might still be incorrect but include at least one letter for every sound (e.g. *sed/said, pecos/because, rynoserus/ rhinoceros*). Finally, when spelling is correct, the specific patterns and rules of English have been absorbed – we say that full orthographic competence has been reached. According to this model, it is *dysphonetic spelling*, where the sequence of letters does not reflect the order of sounds in the spoken word, which would raise initial concerns.

We might also use the model to analyse single-word reading skills. We would expect sight recognition and phonic decoding skills to be eventually joined by the use of analogy to known words and use of context. Where readers do not develop this full range of strategies, or rely too heavily on just one, it will be more difficult to read well.

However, reading is much more than recognising single words. Its purpose is to gain *meaning* from text. The skills required for this higher-level task can be thought of as a combination of 'top-down' and 'bottom-up' processes, skills and abilities.

- The top-down processes are those the reader brings to the text which are rooted in spoken language skills: vocabulary and grammatical knowledge, the ability to infer from context and predict what is coming next, the use of general knowledge to add to and/or check for meaning and sense.
- The bottom-up processes refer to the ability to decode the letters on the page.

Effective top-down processes can compensate for weaker bottom-up skills. For example, good spoken language skills and the ability to use context to self-correct when reading can compensate for poor word recognition.

Assessing **listening comprehension** is one valuable way of disentangling the underlying causes of reading comprehension difficulty. Good decoding skills but poor listening comprehension may be seen in children with general learning difficulties; excellent listening comprehension but poor decoding skills may be observed in cases of dyslexia. However, both groups might have weaknesses in reading comprehension – particularly when speed is taken into account, which might apply in SpLDs such as dyslexia.

Summary

■ Spoken language skills and phonological awareness underpin effective reading and writing skills.

■ Knowledge of sound-symbol correspondence, and the exceptions to these rules, is needed even for early reading and spelling.

■ Fully efficient single-word reading and spelling skills demand integration of visual, phonic, sub-lexical (morphological) and contextual strategies.

■ Reading success is a combination of language comprehension and single-word reading skills. Individuals might rely on either aspect for some initial success, but as texts become more complex this is likely to be less reliable.

Dyslexia – definitions and descriptions

What is dyslexia? We need an answer to this question if we are to identify it in a reliable fashion. Yet debate continues about the nature of dyslexia. Even a brief review of academic literature quickly reveals a wide range of definitions and descriptions, alongside a selection of alternate causal models.

However, the very significant distance travelled in research can provide a firm platform from which to go forward. A consensus is established that **deficits in phonological abilities** are at the core of dyslexia and are recognised as a defining feature. This is not to say that no other aspects of cognition are involved – but more is known and understood about this aspect than others.

Weaknesses in phonological abilities are central to the following working definition of dyslexia included in an influential review, led by Sir Jim Rose,[3] which has been widely accepted in the UK:

– *Dyslexia is a learning difficulty that primarily affects the skills involved in accurate and fluent word reading and spelling.*

– *Characteristic features of dyslexia are difficulties in phonological awareness, verbal memory and verbal processing speed.*

– *Dyslexia occurs across the range of intellectual abilities. It is best thought of as a continuum, not a distinct category, and there are no clear cut-off points.*

– *Co-occurring difficulties may be seen in aspects of language, motor coordination, mental calculation, concentration and personal organisation, but these are not, by themselves, markers of dyslexia.*

– *A good indication of the severity and persistence of dyslexic difficulties can be gained by examining how the individual responds or has responded to well-founded intervention.*

---

[3] DCSF (2009) *Identifying and Teaching Children and Young People with Dyslexia and Literacy Difficulties (Rose Report)*, DCSF.

Some organisations have extended this definition to include difficulties in **visual processing** as characteristic of dyslexia – encompassing the accuracy and speed of working with detailed visual information such as letters, numbers and other symbols.

Looking more widely, the most influential definitions of specific difficulties internationally are those included in the *Diagnostic and Statistical Manual of Mental Disorders* (DSM-V)[4] – although terms such as 'dyslexia' are not used. A diagnosis can be made when skills are significantly below average and cannot be explained by other factors influencing learning – such as intelligence, education or other sensory impairment.

Definitions provide a benchmark against which we evaluate our assessment data so they are crucial. They also influence decisions about assessment practice – what tests to include, what questions to ask – and all show that assessors need to consider a broad range of potential influences on development. These influences have been captured succinctly in the well-known causal modelling framework[5] which sets out three levels of description – biological, cognitive and behavioural – and highlights that environmental factors have an impact on each. Frith (2002)[6] discusses how this model can be used to show the links between apparently competing theories of dyslexia, the co-occurrence of difficulties and the substantial differences between individuals.

Environment	Brain (*the biological level*)
	Mind (*the cognitive level*)
	Behaviour (*the behavioural level*)

Let us now explore dyslexia at the levels set out in this model and consider how such knowledge informs and structures our assessment procedures.

Biological level

Brain-imaging techniques have been widely employed to show the functional differences between the brains of those with and without specific difficulties. Research also continues into the genetic basis of all the specific learning difficulties. This suggests that there is no single gene for dyslexia, or any other SpLD: multiple genes are involved, and even if a genetic predisposition exists, this does not mean the effect is certain – our genetic make-up can change in response to both internal and external environmental factors – and outcomes are a result of a *combination* of risk factors.

At present, the most useful information for assessors at the biological level of analysis is that specific learning difficulties tend to run in families. If a parent or

---

[4] American Psychiatric Association (2013) *Diagnostic and Statistical Manual of Mental Disorders*, 5th edition, American Psychiatric Association.

[5] Morton, J. and Frith, U. (1995) 'Causal modelling: A structural approach to developmental psychopathology', in *Manual of Developmental Psychopathology*, Cicchetti, D. and Cohen, D. J. (Eds), Wiley.

[6] Frith, U. (2002) 'Resolving the Paradoxes of Dyslexia', in *Dyslexia and Literacy: Theory and Practice*, Reid, G. and Wearmouth, J. (Eds), Wiley.

grandparent or sibling is known to have a difficulty, there is a greater likelihood that others in the family might face similar problems. Therefore, assessors can usefully include questions that ask sensitively about any family history of difficulties and can let individuals know about the heritable nature of SpLDs.

Cognitive level

Analysis at the cognitive level is central to the assessment of SpLDs. **Cognition** refers to the processes of the mind, and in assessment we aim to build a picture of individual cognitive abilities, although we should recognise that no combination of tests could capture the full range of talents, skills and aptitudes that an individual might possess. For our purpose, we look into a core set of capacities linked to phonology, memory, speed of processing and verbal and non-verbal abilities.

Phonological abilities

As shown in Figure 1.2, phonological abilities are a set of skills which must work together if literacy is to be fully efficient; weaknesses in this area are established as a key explanatory factor in the difficulties of dyslexia.

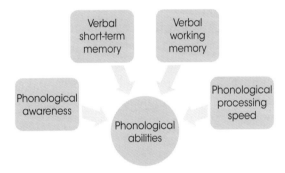

Figure 1.2

A deficit in **phonological awareness** prevents young learners with dyslexia from identifying the sounds in spoken words. Phonological awareness can be improved with teaching, although the impact of a delay, and any lack of automaticity, can continue to hamper fully efficient progress. We discussed the development of phonological awareness earlier in this chapter. In considering SpLDs, it will always be useful to review how far along the path of phonological development an individual has travelled.

Working memory

Weaknesses in **memory** are also noted in the Rose definition of dyslexia. This does not refer to a weakness in long-term memory but in *working* memory, and specifically in the verbal aspects. Therefore, it is helpful for assessors to look to a model of working memory to support their practice.

Working memory is the system which allows us to hold on to and manipulate information in our minds. For everyone, this system has limited capacity and duration – small amounts of information can be held only for a very short time. In cases of SpLDs, this capacity is characteristically reduced and working memory weaknesses or inefficiencies are known to have a significant impact.

We need efficient working memories for many everyday tasks, particularly all those that require multi-tasking – from taking a telephone message, to calculating change, to following directions, and all manner of complex cognitive activities. In school, working memory is needed to listen and write at the same time, to follow a text being read aloud, to join in a discussion, to follow a list of spoken instructions, to copy from the board and so on. Reading comprehension and writing composition make substantial demands on working memory. When placed in stressful situations or when anxiety goes beyond a manageable level, working memory capacity will be reduced as it devotes energy to managing the anxiety rather than the task in hand.

Gathercole and Packiam-Alloway (2008)[7] set out a model to summarise the main components of the working memory system, drawing on the seminal work of Baddeley (1986)[8]. It shows working memory has three key parts that must operate together: the central executive, the verbal short-term memory and the visual-spatial short-term memory – see Figure 1.3.[9]

The short-term memory simply holds information without further action and works through the central executive to complete any higher-level task beyond simple recall.

- The verbal short-term memory stores any material that can be expressed in spoken language, for example numbers, words and sentences.
- The visual-spatial short-term memory is concerned with images, pictures and locations.

Weaknesses in working memory are known to be highly prevalent in SpLDs and this is a key area of testing. Differentiating between visual and verbal memory abilities might be illuminating to decide on the character of difficulties.

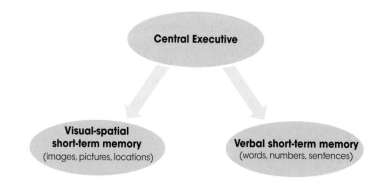

Figure 1.3

[7] Gathercole, S. E. and Packiam-Alloway, T. (2008) *Working Memory and Learning: a practical guide for teachers*, Sage.

[8] Baddeley, A. D. (1986) *Working Memory*, Oxford University Press.

[9] Readers might be familiar with Baddeley's terminology for these short-term memory stores: the phonological loop and the visual-spatial sketchpad.

Executive function

The whole working memory system is part of a wider group of higher-order cognitive activities known as *executive functions*. They are a crucial and complex set of inter-related abilities which we use every day and include, for example, the ability to:

- select a focus for attention or maintain, shift, or divide attention, when needed;
- plan and organise;
- control impulses;
- be flexible in our thinking;
- apply past learning to new situations;
- make decisions;
- break complex problems into smaller components;
- process information.

This list will strike a chord with specialist teachers who will recognise these as areas of difficulty for some of their pupils. Impaired executive function might partly explain the problems with, for example, concentration, time management, organisation and that inability to apply information learned today to the task tomorrow, which we often observe in cases of SpLDs. Weaknesses in executive functions have been most notably studied in relation to ADHD, but a relationship with *all* learning difficulties seems likely, although research is at an early stage. While tests of executive function are available, their validity is debated. Specialist assessors must proceed with significant caution and are advised to stay informed about this developing area of understanding.

Phonological processing speed

The final contributor to the overall picture of phonological abilities is **phonological processing speed**, also known as **verbal processing speed**.

This refers to how quickly information expressed in spoken language (letters, words, sentences) can be retrieved. We need good phonological processing speed for success in a wide range of tasks, and weakness here leads to several characteristic difficulties for those with dyslexia and wider SpLDs. These might extend to, for example, the ability to bring to mind the words we wish to say, to give names to the things and people we see, to read quickly or spell fluently (through quickly applying the phonological codes to the letters on the page), or to work efficiently with sequences of any kind.

To test phonological processing speed, rapid-naming tasks are most often used. The words to name – for example, familiar letters, numbers, shapes, objects or colours – must be found and articulated at speed. Rapid-naming abilities in young children have been found to be very good predictors of later reading success.

Weakness in phonological abilities: wider impact

Inefficient or impaired abilities in storing, retrieving and manipulating sounds can lead to a number of experiences which are considered to be characteristic diagnostic features of dyslexia. If observed, or reported, they provide some qualitative evidence to support conclusions.

Vocabulary acquisition might be restricted. To learn new words efficiently, we use secure knowledge of the word's sound sequence and link it to the meaning. If this process is impaired, learning is likely to be slower. Also, as reading experience contributes to vocabulary knowledge as children grow older, the underlying phonological deficit makes gaining such experience that much harder.

Delayed speech is frequently noted in a child who is at risk of dyslexia. Later, **speech errors** and mispronunciations might be observed, as the sound sequences within words are not completely represented in the mind.

Word-finding difficulties are common in dyslexia and some other SpLDs. This is where the sounds of a word cannot be quickly retrieved, or the wrong word is used (*boot* might be retrieved instead of *shoe*, for example).

Quick access to the *sounds* of words contributes to understanding why **reading aloud** is far harder for many with dyslexia, in comparison to reading silently. Reading aloud can be prone to error and lacking fluency, with little retention of meaning. Weak phonological processing also partly explains ongoing problems **remembering sequences** – for example, days/weeks/months, or the alphabet, or times tables.

Visual processing speed

There is another key type of processing speed useful in assessment of SpLD – where demands are placed mostly in the visual domain. **Visual processing speed** tasks require rapid work with information which is less easily labelled verbally. Tests usually involve working with unfamiliar shapes and symbols. Weaknesses here contribute to other characteristics in the SpLD profile. They have an impact on reading and writing speed (in conjunction with phonological aspects) but might also influence a range of other tasks, such as the ability to work with mathematical notation, or to analyse diagrams quickly, or the ability to work quickly and efficiently with visual information generally. For example, assessors might see difficulties emerge in reading as an inability to take note of the small details in words and a reliance on whole-word strategies. There might also be difficulties in identifying detail in pictures and diagrams, particularly in time-pressured situations.

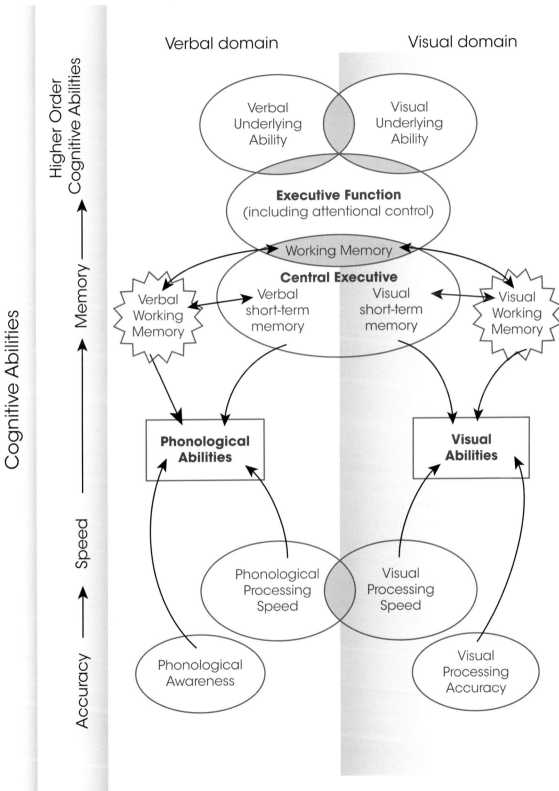

Figure 1.4   Simplified representation of verbal/visual assessment domains

Visual stress

Visual difficulties can also emerge where text appears unstable despite apparently unimpaired vision – this is often known as **visual stress** or **Meares-Irlen Syndrome**. Some individuals with SpLDs report tendencies for words to move, word spacing to vary and text to blur. However, these difficulties can exist without any SpLD but would clearly prevent easy reading, so these factors need to be considered in assessments.

Underlying abilities

As assessors, we would not be doing our job if we did not look beyond SpLDs to see if other cognitive factors were relevant to the presenting problem. Clearly, a certain level of underlying ability is needed for successful learning, and if it is age-appropriate, the potential to cope with normal literacy and study-related activities should exist, all other things being equal. Reflecting models of intelligence, we investigate underlying abilities in the verbal domain – typically the knowledge and use of language – alongside those in the non-verbal domain, which give a view of logical thinking and problem-solving skills. A few key points regarding underlying ability are worth noting here:

1. Studies have generally shown relatively low correlations (0.4–0.6) between IQ test results and examination grades – so we should never underestimate the contribution that good teaching and hard work can make to educational achievement, nor overestimate the significance of underlying ability scores.

2. We know that all SpLDs can affect people right across the ability range. However, assessors must be cautious as those individuals with general difficulties in learning also tend to show the characteristic processing weaknesses of specific difficulties. If weaknesses exist across the cognitive profile, it is unlikely that a specific difficulty is the best explanation of any presenting literacy problems.

3. Verbal ability, in particular, is considered to be of greater significance for the smooth development of higher-level skills (comprehension and composition) than for mastering the basic decoding process, although it is a good compensatory factor at all stages.

Behavioural level

Analysis at the behavioural level investigates the impact of any cognitive weaknesses on the individual, including reading, writing, spelling, and numeracy. It is worth noting, however, that as we are taking a developmental view, the nature of what we see here will vary greatly – often with age, but also for every individual. For example, in dyslexia, what starts out as a phonics/word-level problem might begin to look different as a child grows older. Even if these skills become reasonably secure, the difficulty and delay in developing phonological skills might have had a lasting effect and prevent the development of efficient higher-level literacy skills, such as reading comprehension or well-structured writing. Similarly, in dyspraxia or ADHD, the difficulties observed change with age, experience and the environment in which individuals find themselves working.

Characteristic behavioural difficulties in dyslexia are to be found in the following areas:

Reading
- Single-word reading accuracy – errors tend to be made in sequencing sounds, sound-symbol correspondence and seeing the detail in words. Unfamiliar words, or non-words, present a particular challenge.
- Reading comprehension – as this activity combines so many skills, a wide range of outcomes might emerge here. Weak reading accuracy and speed might mean comprehension is poor, but good verbal ability and effective reading strategies might compensate so that comprehension is good. In both cases – even the latter – reading comprehension is still likely to be slower and more effortful than expected.
- Reading speed – working quickly is a fundamental difficulty in dyslexia.

Writing
- Spelling – difficulties tend to persist both in accuracy and fluency. Surprising errors might continue to appear in straightforward common words, even when skills are improving. Accurate spelling might need several attempts and interrupt the process of writing.
- Composition – the combination of underlying difficulties means that writing accurately, fluently and efficiently might prove the most difficult task for those with dyslexia. Work might be poorly structured, and show errors in grammar, punctuation and spelling, although the quality of ideas and creativity might be good and/or demonstrate good subject knowledge. Writing speed is likely to be slow.

Beyond literacy

Returning to the 'Rose' definition of dyslexia, we see that it refers to other characteristic difficulties which commonly co-occur beyond reading and writing skills. Therefore, in building an individual profile, assessors will investigate the following:
- Motor coordination weaknesses – these might extend to both fine and/or gross motor difficulties. Problems in handwriting might emerge or individuals might report some problems with balance, spatial awareness or movement. In cases where motor coordination difficulties are persistent and significant, dyspraxia might be worthy of consideration.
- Organisation and time-keeping difficulties.
- Directional confusion, the tendency to be easily lost in new places, problems using maps.

- Lack of confidence in mathematics – word problems and learning sequences are particularly difficult, although maths can be an area of strength for some with dyslexia.
- Problems maintaining concentration and attention.

Strengths

The behavioural level of analysis must of course not be limited to difficulties, problems and weaknesses: compensatory or additional strengths should always be considered. They might relate directly to the use of language (perhaps in good spoken language skills) but, whatever their nature, they can contribute to successful learning. Their identification is as much a part of a good assessment as anything else.

Environmental level

Finally, we turn to environmental influences on development. They operate at every level – biological, cognitive and behavioural – and are far reaching. Assessors will have to explore how they might have had an impact on the assessment results, and weigh up all the evidence carefully before concluding an SpLD is present. We discuss this in much more detail in Chapter 5, but investigations will include, at a minimum, factors relating to physical and mental health, vision and hearing, developmental history, the linguistic environment, and social and educational experience.

For example, a child who 'missed the boat' through poor attendance, illness, emotional or behavioural difficulties, or poor teaching during crucial 'learning the code' years, can seem to have difficulties similar to dyslexia at 7–8 years old and will certainly need help. However, he may not have an SpLD and, in such cases, skills can steadily improve once appropriate extra support is put in place. Another case might be where an older student describes typical dyslexia-type problems in note-taking and extended essay writing, but if this is the first time they have met these demands and they have received no direct teaching in study skills, they would naturally find these tasks difficult.

Diagnostic conclusion: dyslexia or not?

The question is how to bring all this information together when drawing a diagnostic conclusion. We suggest assessors look to the wide assessment profile, including both quantitative and qualitative data. To conclude that dyslexia is present, assessors might test their findings against the following criteria.

- Is there a marked inefficiency in cognitive processing abilities – specifically phonological awareness, verbal memory, and/or slow processing speeds?
- Do these weaknesses have a clear, substantial and persisting impact on reading and writing skills?
- Are the cognitive processing and literacy weaknesses notable and unexpected in light of the individual's wider cognitive profile and case history?

■ Can other factors relating to educational, developmental or medical factors be excluded as reasons for any difficulties?

The final decision is not, of course, as straightforward as it looks here. Every individual with dyslexia will experience it in a different way, and no two individuals will have exactly the same story, as a result of their different life and educational experiences. The skilled assessor will look to core features and patterns of co-occurring characteristics to come to each conclusion.

Social model of specific learning difficulties

To date, most of the work surrounding dyslexia adopts a medical model of disability and suggests there is a 'within-person' explanation for any difficulties. It implies there is something wrong with the individual – they have a deficit or disorder – which gives rise to symptoms demanding intervention and treatment. These are all very medically-related terms.

The social model of disability takes a radically different view, where the source of the disability is not the individual but the society within which the person lives. It does not deny the reality of the difficulties, but highlights that how they are experienced depends on much wider factors. Certainly, in non-literate societies an inability to spell would not be the subject of such concern as it is in ours!

As assessors we cannot solve the dilemma between the medical and social models, but we can address both aspects. We can take a view that while the individual does experience a 'difference' in their biological and cognitive make-up, we can agree that their environment makes a very great difference to the degree of effect it has on them. Therefore, when making recommendations, we should consider not just the steps the individual could take to build his skills and develop strategies, but also the adjustments to be made to reduce the negative impact of the context.

Other SpLDs, co-occurrence and labelling

It is well established that specific difficulties commonly overlap and therefore assessors need a broad working knowledge of wider SpLD profiles. In complex cases, of dyslexia or other difficulties, it is always helpful to work and liaise with colleagues and other professionals.

The research base in other SpLDs is often less well established than in dyslexia. In the following discussion, you will soon see that core cognitive difficulties are sometimes less explicitly understood and definitions rely more heavily on the description of behavioural characteristics. We will consider the most common diagnostic categories in turn, before returning at the end of this chapter to the issue of co-occurrence and the challenges of providing individuals with diagnostic labels.

Dyspraxia

Dyspraxia in children is formally diagnosed by medical practitioners, occupational therapists, physiotherapists or other professional members of child development teams – although teachers are very often instrumental in making initial referrals. The definition below was agreed when representatives of these professions met education colleagues to approve an approach that all UK practitioners could use. The aim was to ensure the medical and educational needs of individuals with dyspraxia were considered, wherever they were assessed. The definition is as follows:

> *'Developmental Coordination Disorder (DCD), also known as Dyspraxia in the UK, is a common disorder affecting fine or gross motor coordination in children and adults. This lifelong condition is formally recognised by international organisations including the World Health Organisation. DCD is distinct from other motor disorders such as cerebral palsy and stroke and occurs across the range of intellectual abilities. Individuals may vary in how their difficulties present; these may change over time depending on environmental demands and life experience.*
>
> *'An individual's coordination difficulties may affect participation and functioning of everyday life skills in education, work and employment. Children may present with difficulties with self-care, writing, typing, riding a bike and play as well as other educational and recreational activities. In adulthood many of these difficulties will continue, as well as learning new skills at home, in education and work, such as driving a car and DIY. There may be a range of co-occurring difficulties which can also have serious negative impacts on daily life. These include social and emotional difficulties as well as problems with time management, planning and personal organisation and these may also affect an adult's education or employment experiences.'*

This definition clearly locates dyspraxia as a difficulty of motor coordination. It is not a mild issue of a clumsy child, or a badly organised teenager, or an individual with illegible handwriting, but a substantial and persistent difficulty that might encompass all these difficulties and more. Further guidance which accompanied this definition is available on the Patoss website.

For the assessor, this provides some clear direction as to typical characteristics:

- A detailed background history of difficulty in motor coordination is essential. This will include delayed development of gross and fine motor skills in the early years, although some difficulties might be overcome in adulthood through practice, just as reading and writing skills can improve in those with dyslexia. Do note that any recent or rapid deterioration in motor function should prompt a medical referral.
- Difficulties are very likely to include handwriting. Letters might be poorly formed or illegible, pen grip and pressure on the page might be inappropriate. Writing is likely to be slow and keyboard skills difficult to master. Layout of written work and maths (execution of diagrams, etc) might be of a low standard.

- Planning and organisation difficulties of all kinds might be observed. This applies to movement – reaching out to pick up a cup, or using scissors, tripping up stairs, spilling or dropping things – but also to thought and language – for example, organising ideas for writing, deciding how long activities will take or scheduling a day's activities.
- Direction and orientation tend to present ongoing difficulties, sometimes even in familiar locations.
- Speech difficulties might exist – individuals might have been late learning to talk and some articulation difficulties can persist.
- Maths is a common, although certainly not universal, difficulty in cases of dyspraxia, partly because of the demands on visual-spatial skills.

Dyscalculia

Although the term *dyscalculia* has moved into reasonably common use in educational circles, full understanding is far behind that of dyslexia, and there are no agreed criteria for diagnosis. One frequently quoted definition says that:

> *'Dyscalculia is a condition that affects the ability to acquire arithmetical skills. Dyscalculic learners may have difficulty understanding simple number concept, lack an intuitive grasp of numbers, and have problems learning number facts and procedures. Even if they produce a correct answer or use a correct method, they may do so mechanically and without confidence'.*[10]

Moving this forward, Chinn (2004)[11] has added other aspects of dyscalculia – the tendency of difficulties to persist despite appropriate teaching; the difficulties of understanding the value of numbers and the inter-relationships between them; and the difficulty of retrieving number facts quickly, even if they have been successfully learned. In practice this means an individual with dyscalculia is likely to have difficulties not only with arithmetic, but also with handling abstract concepts such as time, as well as everyday measures such as money, temperature and speed, and spatial concepts (left/right orientation is often not mastered). Fundamentally, working with mathematical information of all kinds is difficult, even at what appears to be elementary levels of functioning. A key feature throughout is the very slow speed of work, as well as its possible surprising inaccuracy.

This is a useful description, but the underlying neuro-cognitive profile is not yet clear. Some researchers suggest dyscalculia is fundamentally an inability to recognise small numerosities – the number of things in a small set – without counting; a lack of number sense. Others suggest this might be one of many factors alongside weaknesses in visual-spatial abilities and working memory systems. The assessor can look out for these features, but a further complication is the common occurrence of maths *anxiety*, which is unrelated to intelligence or aptitude, but which makes learning the subject exceptionally difficult.

---

[10] DfES (2001) *The National Numeracy Strategy: guidance to support pupils with dyslexia and dyscalculia*, DfES.

[11] Chinn, S. (2004) *The Trouble With Maths – a practical guide to helping learners with numeracy difficulties*, Routledge Falmer.

The key to any diagnostic decision is in the case history and the early and persisting nature of difficulty. Therefore, the assessment task is complex and demands – once again – thorough research into the background to investigate impartially the potential reasons for current difficulties and to exclude environmental factors.

Of course, not everyone who has difficulties in numbers will have dyscalculia. Linguistic difficulties associated with dyslexia can affect the development of numeracy. Visual-spatial problems can also cause problems in this subject. Attention difficulties might prevent learning. Any of these might be the chief cause of problems – not a separate specific mathematical difficulty.

Attention deficit hyperactivity disorder

Difficulties in maintaining attention and concentration are found commonly across the spectrum of SpLDs, but if there are significant and pervasive problems, assessors should be aware of the possibility of **Attention Deficit Hyperactivity Disorder** (ADHD) so they can take appropriate steps and make referrals for further assessment.

ADHD is the acronym accepted by the National Institute for Health and Care Excellence (NICE), the British Medical Association and the American Psychiatric Association (publisher of *The Diagnostic and Statistical Manual of Mental Disorders*, DSM-V), and others. It is now the formal diagnostic term to include those with or without features of hyperactivity.

ADHD is classified as a neurodevelopmental disorder and the NICE guidelines (2008) cover diagnosis and treatment. The key characteristics of ADHD are related to impulsivity and inattentiveness, and can occur with or without elements of physical or mental hyperactivity. It is characterised by a pattern of behaviour, present in multiple domains (e.g. school/work and home), that have a significant impact on activities in everyday life. The DSM-V definition gives a detailed list of symptoms for children and adults which indicate the possible presence of ADHD. This information is widely available on the Internet, but the following are of particular note:

- Some difficulties must have been evident by the age of 12 years.
- There must be evidence of significant impairment of functioning over time.
- Difficulties cannot be better explained by other conditions or circumstances.

While ADHD is described in terms of behaviour, it can also be categorised as a cognitive disorder, and substantial knowledge does exist about underlying biological and cognitive factors. Firstly, brain-imaging and genetic studies have demonstrated the neurological basis of the difficulty. In the cognitive domain, weaknesses in executive function have been linked to ADHD. These relate to weakness in the central executive function of working memory and the inability to inhibit a response and postpone gratification. Also, weaknesses in processing speed are common in ADHD, and although individuals might seem to be always 'on-the-go', they can have significant difficulties working quickly, particularly in academically related tasks.

Once again, a detailed understanding of the individual background history is needed, with information gathered from a wide range of sources and settings. Assessors should be cautious only to work within their areas of expertise and seek referrals as necessary. If school is the *only* place where concentration cannot be maintained, the problem certainly lies elsewhere!

Specific language impairment

Awareness of **specific language impairment** (SLI) is much less widespread than dyslexia, although its prevalence is similar and there is a firm base of understanding of the associated cognitive difficulties.

An SLI is a difficulty in understanding and using spoken language. It can emerge in receptive language, the ability to understand what has been said, and/or in expressive language, the ability to put words together to form spoken sentences. Such problems mean that using language appropriately is not easy. Communication in social situations can be particularly difficult and many children with language problems experience literacy difficulties.

The difficulties associated with SLI will most likely include these key categories:
- Phonology – in common with dyslexia, difficulties in phonological awareness and verbal memory. In some cases there might also be difficulties with articulation and word-finding.
- Vocabulary – individuals find it difficult to develop an age-appropriate vocabulary.
- Grammar (syntax and morphology) – difficulties emerge in the accurate use of grammatical rules to build sentences, especially longer and more complex constructions. Assessors might note, for example, particular problems with using the correct word order, word form or with using the wrong tense. These difficulties are likely to appear in both conversation and writing.
- Semantics and pragmatics – characteristic difficulties include understanding word meanings in context, combining language with non-verbal communication (such as expression, tone of voice), and using and understanding metaphors and idioms. Using language in social situations is particularly problematic.

As in all skills, children develop at different rates.[12] Some children with weak language skills are simply late developers, especially if they have not had adequate opportunity to begin building these skills before entering school. They will catch up even though they show a delay in development. However, if development is evidently far behind normal expectations, an SLI might be suspected, and referral to a speech and language therapist should be considered.

However, once again, cautions abound. Individuals experiencing hearing difficulties, general learning difficulties and autistic spectrum disorders often have language difficulties. There is also a good deal in common with dyslexia,

---

[12] For information on the normal development of spoken language skills, alongside a range of other professional resources, see **The Communication Trust** at www.thecommunicationtrust.org.uk. Further very useful information is available at www.ican.org.uk and www.afasicengland.org.uk (also, see Afasic Scottish, Welsh and Irish websites).

and the distinction might not be clear. One key difference is in the ability to use spoken language – often a strength in dyslexia, but those with SLI do not have this to fall back on – thus information from those who know the individual well will be needed to explore the nature of their language difficulties.

Other unusual profiles

Beyond the widely used diagnostic labels discussed above, two other profiles are emerging as areas of interest. These relate to difficulties which are limited to **writing composition** and **reading comprehension**. We introduce them here to alert assessors to research, but advise very substantial caution in practice. Assessors must look broadly and thoroughly to understand the individual fully.

Written composition difficulties

There are young people and adults whose reading skills, spoken language skills, gross motor skills and general knowledge and abilities are entirely as we might expect, but who face inordinate difficulties in producing written text. The forming and spacing of letters is difficult, as is overall layout and presentation. Writing is produced only with substantial effort and very slowly, and the result is largely illegible, with context needed in many cases to decipher words. In addition, there might be spelling difficulties even when phonological skills are strong, due to weakness in the motor coordination aspect of the task. However, it is not just physical aspects of handwriting which are weak, but also underlying cognitive processing abilities and visual-motor integration skills. In clear cases, where the impairment is very specific to handwriting with relevant processing weaknesses, the diagnostic label of **dysgraphia** might be one to consider.

Again, it is important to be cautious. Handwriting difficulties characterise many other profiles and there is no need to use a further diagnostic label. Those with dyslexia tend also to have weaknesses here, and where there are wider motor coordination difficulties, dyspraxia is likely to be a more useful conclusion. Weak handwriting can of course also be a matter of poor teaching, lack of practice (especially with increasing reliance on word processing), a case of slower development, or simply carelessness or haste – all of which can be overcome. It is when substantial difficulties persist in spite of continued effort that concerns might first be raised.

Reading comprehension difficulties

Often called 'poor comprehenders', the needs of this group of learners can easily be missed if assessors take a limited view of literacy difficulties and focus only on word-level concerns.[13] Their difficulties are complex and most likely based in weaknesses in language. A key characteristic is that word-reading skills are intact – with good phonological abilities, word reading accuracy and speed – but this does not translate into effective reading comprehension.

---

[13] For a very useful review, see Cain, K. (2010) *Reading Development and Difficulties*, BPS Blackwell.

The difficulties centre on an inability to knit together word meanings. Good readers build pictures of meaning from successive sentences, integrate them all, make inferences where necessary (they read between the lines), and monitor their own understanding throughout. It is these tasks that prove difficult.

However, research continues and the profile is not clear and so assessors are well advised to be extremely cautious before deciding reading comprehension is a specific weakness – this characteristic could very easily be part of another specific difficulty or none. For example, a lack of general knowledge, and/or general learning difficulties, will also mean scores achieved in measures of reading comprehension are low. Single-word reading might be secure because this task is simpler and individuals with weaker abilities find reading comprehension too difficult. In addition, reading comprehension weaknesses might be due to lack of effective reading experience and a subsequent failure to build the skills which are normally gained from text – we must read in order to become effective readers!

Also, the individual who has substantially compensated for the word-level difficulties associated with dyslexia or a specific language impairment might still struggle to combine automatically all the skills necessary for efficient reading comprehension.

Co-occurrence: the new norm

Having considered individual diagnostic categories we return now to the issue of overlapping difficulties.

In the past, a simple one-to-one relationship was often employed to reach a conclusion, where a particular cognitive difference led to a particular outcome. However, current approaches acknowledge that the situation is much more complicated. The outcome for an individual is seen as a consequence of a complex interaction of multiple risk factors, including genetic influences, cognitive weaknesses and life experiences. We readily accept this in matters of physical health and it seems logical that it can also apply to developmental, biologically-based difficulties such as SpLDs.

Hulme and Snowling (2009)[14] have concluded that entirely 'pure' cases of a single SpLD are unlikely, although not impossible, and as research continues, it is clear that very many overlaps exist. To capture the wide range of experiences, strengths, weaknesses and difficulties in a different way, the concept of neuro-diversity is receiving increasing attention. This approach recognises core cognitive differences but acknowledges that they are experienced in multiple and various combinations, leading to different individual outcomes. Essentially, as human beings are diverse in their physical make-up, so they are diverse in their cognitive make-up and there is an infinite variety of combinations.

---

[14] Hulme, C. and Snowling, M. J. (2009) *Developmental Disorders of Language, Learning and Cognition.* Wiley-Blackwell.

Specialist assessors are likely to recognise readily all those neuro-diverse cases where a child or adult does not fit neatly or comfortably into a single diagnostic box. This conceptualisation of SpLD does have very far-reaching implications for assessment, however, especially if working in an educational or employment context which demands that a diagnostic label is stated.

Diagnostic labels

It is undeniable that many individuals and their families find a diagnostic label comforting, reassuring and helpful – many report they would not have received any support without the recognition that a label brings. However, a question arises as to how to move forward if an assessor observes multiple difficulties, or an unusual combination of difficulties in an individual. A long list of diagnostic labels can prove entirely dispiriting and confusing.

Here the diagnostic conclusion of 'an SpLD' can be very useful, along with a descriptive approach that specifies the strengths and weaknesses of the profile. The individual might well ask, *'Am I dyslexic or not?'* This is understandable given the wider familiarity with this label over others – but our job is to share our understanding of the overlapping nature of difficulties and neuro-diversity to give individuals some language to describe their circumstances to others. We might say individuals have features of particular conditions but highlight that this does not mean they have multiple disabilities – simply that they have a unique profile. As we know that no two individuals ever experience exactly the same outcome, being 'unique' is common in the world of SpLD.

All assessors will be acutely aware of the responsibility of 'labelling' anyone and, whatever the approach, any diagnostic name or label should simply be a pre-cursor to a description of the individual's difficulties and strengths which helps him understand his past experience and manage the impact in the future.

2 Basic Concepts in Psychometrics

This chapter presents a brief summary of some of the most important issues to understand when choosing and using psychometric tests. These provide us with the statistical data which we need to build a firm conclusion. In the story of an assessment, these statistics are the bones of the plot, and using them confidently will make for more firmly grounded analysis. We will look at the following areas:

- The standard normal distribution and two key statistics derived from it: the mean and standard deviation;
- Criteria for choosing tests: the standardisation sample, reliability and validity;
- Measurement error: the imperfect nature of tests and confidence intervals;
- Key data in using tests: test scores and descriptors;
- Approaches to score comparisons and using statistically significant differences and prevalence.

The normal distribution

Measurements of human characteristics, *when taken from a sufficiently large sample*, conform very well to a pattern known as a 'normal distribution'. As we use this theory to underpin all the comparisons we make in diagnostic assessment, it is essential to understand it and its application.

If asked to define 'normal' in everyday life, we might reply that it is what we expect to see most of the time, although we know there is always variation; this commonsense view is a good way to think about a 'normal distribution'. It describes measures across a population and assumes that the majority of people tend to be clustered within an average range in terms of attributes – height, weight or cognitive abilities, for example – with far fewer at the extremes. Represented graphically, it produces a smooth, symmetrical curve with known mathematical properties and the familiar bell shape.

The central point of the distribution is the **mean** – the arithmetical average score for the reference group on whom the test was standardised – but we also need to know how scores are *spread* around this average: are all scores close to the average or are they widely dispersed? To measure this variation in the scatter of scores, another statistic is calculated: the **standard deviation**. The standard deviation is the 'average' amount by which scores differ from the mean, regardless of direction.

The bell-shaped distribution (Figure 2.1) is then sliced into four vertical parts which are each one standard deviation wide. The graph represents the whole population (100%) and the area under the curve covered by each slice represents a fixed proportion of it.

■ The area betwcen -1 and +1 standard deviations of the mean represents 68% of the population – with 34% either side of the mean.
■ The area between -2 and + 2 standard deviations represents 95% of the population.
■ The area betwcen -3 and + 3 standard deviations represents 99% of the population. Scores achieved beyond this would be very rare.[1]

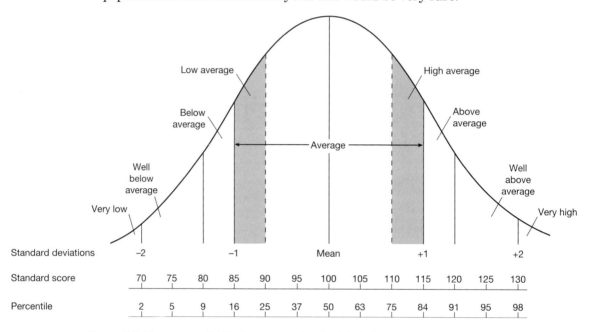

Figure 2.1 The normal distribution curve, standard deviations, standard scores and percentiles

Test developers take one further step to create a 'standardised normal distribution' – essentially a conversion to a common scale – which produces the different types of standardised scores we are accustomed to using in psychometric assessment. We use these scores as they provide a picture against which we can compare the performance of the people we assess – the essence of diagnostic assessment. We shall look in more detail, later in this chapter, at the descriptors and scales shown in this graph. But let us first turn to the practical application of this theory: the choosing and using of the tests which measure these normally distributed skills.

Choosing the right tests

Before we use *any* test, we should check to see if it meets our purpose well. The test should:

---

[1] Please note these values have been rounded up to whole numbers. For instance, for the 95% band, more correctly, the value is 1.96 standard deviations, but by convention, this is rounded to 2.

■ provide a useful benchmark for comparison with the individual we are assessing. The reference group (standardisation sample) must be representative of those assessed. In short, test norms must be relevant;
■ give consistent and accurate results – it must be reliable;
■ measure closely the skill we wish to investigate – it must be valid.

The standardisation sample

Every time we look up an individual's test results in norm tables, we are in effect comparing his performance against the reference group (a sample of the population) used during the test development. The larger that reference group, and the more widely distributed across different people (by age, gender, ethnicity, first language, geographical location, socio-economic status, etc), the more likely it is that the statistics regarding what is average, and above and below average, are meaningful and 'true' for the population as a whole. Tests produced by individuals or small organisations without the resources or expertise needed to support proper test development with large and diverse sample groups should be avoided.

However, the reference group must nevertheless be suitably representative of the individual being assessed. To allow sensible comparisons, as far as possible, it should take into account the appropriate demographic and situational factors. For example, a reference group might specifically include or exclude those in special schools, those with English as an Additional Language or those in Higher Education.

Furthermore, the sample should represent a *recent* profile of the particular population, since language, literacy and other factors are constantly evolving. Norms established several decades ago are much less likely to be fair representations of the population now; they become outdated and scores are subsequently misleading. Equally, if a test item becomes out of date (by virtue of its vocabulary, say), this infringes on the test validity, further undermining the basis of our measurement.

Test age ranges

The age range of the standardisation sample is extremely important – particularly during the primary school years, when development of skills and knowledge is much faster than later on. This is why some tests provide separate norm tables for each six months or sometimes two or three months during the early school years, then expand the age groups to one year or more in the secondary phase. Then, as abilities 'plateau' in adulthood, they are given 5 or 10 year bands.

For statistical reasons, tests do not discriminate well at the *extremes* of the age ranges. Therefore, it is best to use tests where the individual is well within the upper and lower age limits of the test.

If an appropriate test is not available, an assessor might have to use a test for an individual whose chronological age is outside the age range. In these cases, *qualitative* descriptions of performance are best, avoiding statistical language – but if no other data is available, the results might need to be reported formally, although the limitations should be explained. In such cases there should be a good deal of observational and informal evidence to support, or qualify, the test results.

Action: Use recently standardised tests which have been developed using a large and appropriate representative sample.

Action: Wherever possible, choose a test that more than covers the age range of the individual being assessed.

Reliability

There are different ways in which test developers measure test reliability, but we will limit discussion here to three particularly important ones: test-retest, equivalent forms and inter-scorer reliability.

1. If test-retest reliability is good, an individual should obtain a similar score if he takes the test on separate occasions (all other things being equal). Test developers give guidance in manuals about when tests can be reused on the same individual without invalidating the result.

2. If equivalent form reliability is good, an individual should score consistently on parallel[2] forms when retested. We would expect a high coefficient of reliability.

3. If inter-scorer (or assessor) reliability is good, the test should also produce similar results no matter who is administering or marking the test – as long as they are qualified to do so! To support inter-scorer reliability, test developers give very precise test instructions and marking guidelines to remove possible influences on the result which depend on the administration. To preserve the reliability of the test, these instructions, procedures and methods **must** be followed.

The reliability of tests is measured by the degree to which the relationship between variables (for example, two sets of scores) is in accord – that is the degree to which the scores correlate. The actual statistic used is called the 'reliability coefficient'.

Correlation coefficients are used in other areas of statistics as well, and range between minus 1.0 to plus 1.0. For our purposes, the coefficient of reliability of tests should be at least + 0.8 and preferably above + 0.9. The higher the correlation coefficient, the more reliable the test scores are likely to be. A reliability coefficient of 1.0 indicates that when the test was delivered on two separate occasions, the test scores achieved by the standardisation sample corresponded perfectly.

---

[2] Parallel forms are two or more statistically matched versions of a test measuring the same skill or construct.

However, 'perfection' is very unlikely, as 'measurement error' is inherent in psychometric testing. In addition, there are always some unpredictable factors, meaning there is an element of chance which affects every test result. (This is not be confused with avoidable errors – for example, a mistake made by the assessor.) These unpredictable factors might relate to the test situation (perhaps a hot room, or bright lights), how the individual reacts to testing (their energy, attitude, etc), or indeed to the personality and characteristics of the assessor and how this affects the test performance of the person being assessed.

Action: Choose tests with high reliability coefficients.

Action: Deliver tests exactly following standardised instructions.

Validity

There is a range of validity measures and only some types can be determined statistically. For example, 'face' validity, while crucial, is very subjective. Here the responsibility lies with the assessor in making a professional judgement about the suitability of the test for the person being assessed. Is the test 'fair' for them? Are there cultural or emotional factors, for example, which mean it is not appropriate for the particular individual?

Validity must also be considered in the context of what the assessor needs to know: 'content' validity. Does the test really measure what it claims to measure? This might not always be reflected in the test name, therefore familiarity with the precise nature of the test is needed. What skill is being investigated? Does the test do this effectively and precisely? For example, how well does a timed non-word reading test measure phonological awareness? Not well at all. Conversely, how well does the same test measure the ability to combine phonological awareness with phonic decoding at speed? It does this very well indeed.

Comprehensive test manuals will also discuss further underpinning validity issues such as 'construct', 'current' and 'predictive' validity. Predictive validity is of particular interest to assessors. Does, for example, a test of phonological skills provide a reliable indication of expected future acquisition of reading skills, or does GCSE attainment predict performance at HE? Does the test serve any useful purpose if nothing can be predicted from it? *Only tests which can show sound evidence of their validity for their stated purpose, and meet the needs of the individual, should be used.*

Action: Choose a test which focuses clearly on and measures the precise skills under investigation.

Action: Be aware that some tests place multiple demands on individuals and use this knowledge to inform analysis.

Action: Be aware of limitations of tests.

The imperfect nature of tests: confidence intervals

We should reflect our understanding that tests are imperfect and acknowledge that test results will inevitably contain a degree of 'measured skill' plus a degree of 'measurement error'. The hypothetical 'true' score lies somewhere in a range which can be determined. To find this range, we first assume errors are normally distributed and then the standard error of measurement (SEm) can be calculated. The formula for the SEm is given below, although most tests publish this data so it does not have to be calculated. It is useful to see however, as the role of test reliability in this calculation is clear.

$$\text{SEm} = \text{SD } \sqrt{(1-r)}$$

Where SD = standard deviation, r = reliability coefficient of the test

Most test developers use the mathematical properties of the SEm to calculate **confidence intervals**[3] (also sometimes known as a **confidence range** or **band**). Confidence intervals refer to the range of scores, lying above and below the score obtained on the day, within which we can be 'confident' that the individual's 'true' score lies. But how confident do we wish to be?

If we wished to have a range of scores where we were 68% confident that it contained the 'true' score, we would build the range by adding and subtracting one SEm to the score actually obtained. This still leaves a 32% possibility of error beyond the 68%!

Commonly, in psychometric testing, a 68% level of confidence is not considered sufficient and manuals often report 85%, 90%, 95% and 99% levels of confidence. They can be calculated using SEm data. For example, using a range including 2 SEms in either direction away from the obtained score means we can be 95% confident that the true score lies within this wider range. A range including 3 times the SEm would give the 99% confidence interval, where there is only a 1% chance that the true score lies outside this range.

Therefore, the higher the degree of confidence we wish to obtain, the wider will be the range of scores which would include the 'true' score of the person assessed. Assessors should decide in advance which level they wish to use and be consistent.

---

[3] Please note: test publishers might also use a different formula on which to base confidence intervals, one intended to eliminate the effects of regression towards the mean.

Here is an example (with values rounded to whole numbers):

Obtained test score	SEm	68% Confidence Interval	95% Confidence Interval	99% Confidence Interval
90	5	Score ± (1 x SEm) 85–95	Score ± (2 x SEm) 80–100	Score ± (3 x SEm) 75–105

Action: Look up confidence intervals in test manuals. If they are not provided, find the SEm and calculate the confidence interval. They serve as a very useful reminder that scores achieved cannot be taken as absolutes.

Action: Decide, in advance, on an appropriate level of confidence to use. Many assessors choose the 95% level.

Using tests and test scores

Test developers take their raw data and produce tables of 'norms' which tell us about expected performance of specific groups – these are most often groups based on age. A raw score is the actual result achieved on a test: for example, 26 out of 30, or 1 out of 10. As each test has its own scale, raw scores may be meaningless because they cannot be readily compared with other results. Raw scores are therefore converted to derived scores which show each person's position in relation to the reference group.

There are three main types of derived scores: standard scores, percentiles and age-equivalent scores.

Standard scores

These show the individual's position compared to the mean for his age group, and are the most appropriate type of derived score to use when evaluating an overall picture of results.

There are several standardised scales in use in psychometric tests. Many tests use a scale with a mean of 100 and a standard deviation of 15. Another common scale uses a mean of 10 and a standard deviation of three – this is commonly called a 'scaled' score, yet is less precise because of the compression of information. Yet another is a 'T' score, where the mean is 50 and the standard deviation is 10. As the various forms are mathematically equivalent, it is quite acceptable to convert between these scales – see Table 2.1.

To avoid complication for the report user, we recommend assessors limit their use of different types of standardised scores. It is unlikely to be apparent to an individual that a standard score of 85 [mean 100] on one test and a scaled score of 7 [mean 10] on another is actually the same thing! (If converting scores, take great care to be accurate.) It would be appropriate to report all scores as a standard score; some assessors report both standard scores and percentiles but convert scaled scores.

Standard Score Mean = 100	Scaled Score Mean = 10	Percentile Rank / Centile
55	1	0.3
60	2	0.8
65	3	1
70	4	2
75	5	5
80	6	9
85	7	16
90	8	25
95	9	37
100	10	50
105	11	63
110	12	75
115	13	84
120	14	91
125	15	95
130	16	98
135	17	99
140	18	99.2
145	19	99.7

Table 2.1

Percentile ranks/centiles

Percentile ranks, or centiles, relate the score achieved to the performance of those in the standardisation sample and show the percentage of those whose scores fall at the same level or below that of the individual. A 10th percentile rank is therefore a low result (90% would do better) and a 90th percentile rank is very good as only 10% would exceed this score. Note the difference from percentages, which simply refer to the score achieved as a percentage of the maximum possible score.

The 'gap' between various percentiles is not equal and these scores can therefore be misleading. They magnify small differences near the mean which might not be significant. They also reduce the apparent size of large differences near the tails of the curve. Thus the difference, in terms of relative performance, between percentiles of 5 and 15 is far larger than that between percentiles of 45 and 55.

Standard scores avoid this since the intervals on a standardised scale are all equal. (Graphs using percentiles should also be avoided, or used only with great caution, again because of their potential to distort differences.)

Assessors must judge when to use percentiles, and explain them carefully when they do. We recommend reserving them for when a particular point is to be made. It would be a real boost to be told that verbal abilities are in the top 5% of the population; or, if a case needed to be made for support, it might be helpful to highlight that a skill is particularly low.

Age-equivalent scores

The third type of derived score is the **age-equivalent**, such as a reading age. This indicates the chronological age, or age range, of the score achieved, in relation to the mean score of that age group.

However, age-equivalents become less and less appropriate as the age of the individual increases, since the rate of development of skills and attainments slows. For example, a delay of one year in reading age could fall within the average range in a certain age group, and while we might wish to support the individual to build his skills, such a difference is not of itself of immediate diagnostic concern.

It is recommended that age-equivalent scores be avoided altogether. This would certainly apply for all in the secondary and adult age range, but it is preferable not to quote them for children either, as they can be so misleading. If children's teachers, parents or education authorities request an age-equivalent, they should be used with substantial caution, alongside standard scores.

Composite scores

Many tests offer the opportunity to bring together the scores on a number of subtests to provide a composite or index score. The overall score obtained (the composite score) would generally be more reliable than the individual subtest scores and provides a useful overview of a group of related skills. For example, reading accuracy, speed and comprehension might be combined to give a reading composite score; or vocabulary and verbal reasoning brought together to give an overall verbal ability score. However, if a substantial difference exists between subtest scores, combining them to form a composite will hide any underlying strengths and weaknesses, effectively masking the contrasts we are investigating.

Consider the following example for a test of single-word reading efficiency:

Subtest	Sight-word reading	112
	Phonemic decoding (non-word reading)	75
	Composite score	93
If the difference between these two scores was ignored and only the composite used, the very useful information regarding a marked weakness in phonemic decoding, and the relative strength in sight-word recognition, would be lost, as would the opportunity to interpret and explain the difference.		

Therefore, where a statistically significant difference exists between a pair of scores, the assessor might consider it more helpful to maintain the focus on the different scores rather than the composite score, which might hide important diagnostic information. (See later comments on statistical significance.)

Describing scores

It is common practice to give a **descriptive label** to an obtained score, but this is a less straightforward task than might at first appear to be the case. Different test publishers use a variety of labels to describe scores within particular ranges. For example, a score of 86 might be classified as 'below average' in one test, 'average' in another and 'low average' in another. Other words such as poor, weak, low, high, above average and so on are applied in different ways and it can all be very confusing, and even possibly distressing, for the readers of our reports.

As the purpose of a descriptive label is to help report readers, we recommend their needs be given priority when selecting an approach. As there is no general consensus on where cut-off points should lie, a helpful starting point is to think of divisions based on standard deviations, above and below the mean, as shown in the graph on page 26 – see Table 2.2.

Score Range		Suggested Descriptors
131 or more	131+	Very high
116–130	121–130	Well above average / high
	116–120	Above average
85–115	111–115	High average
	90–110	Mid-average
	85–89	Low average
70–84	80–84	Below average
	70–79	Well below average / low
69 or less	69-	Very low

Table 2.2

In diagnostic work it can be helpful to sub-divide these ranges as in Table 2.2. Given the recognised differing views in this area, where assessors use this approach they could include in their reports a note such as: *'Although some manuals use different terms, for the purpose of this report and to aid accessibility for the non-specialist, the labels below are used to describe performance.'*

Given our knowledge of confidence intervals, we must be wary of over-reliance on these labels, as the 'true' score may in fact lie in another category. The use of other non-statistical language in the report commentary might aid understanding. For example, it would be helpful to emphasise the excellence of a score of 128, rather than simply report it as 'well above average'. See Chapter 8 for further discussion and examples.

This classification system, by using a reference to the average, provides an anchor for readers and ensures that the same standard score, in different tests, is described in a consistent way. We want our reports to be understood! It also takes account of approaches adopted by a wide range of test publishers, and avoids unnecessarily negative or vague language.

However, assessors must be aware that for some purposes, notably examination access arrangements, it will be necessary to use the boundaries describing scores as set by those authorities, not the test publisher. If assessors choose to use the descriptors given in test manuals, a chart showing the relationship between each will be needed in the report.

A final note on percentiles: a minor complication arises in that, due to the very different unit of measurement, percentiles do not necessarily correspond precisely with standard scores, and assessors might find apparent inconsistencies when comparing tables in manuals. However, as long as the report is consistent and describes the same relationship between standard scores and percentiles in all tests, this does not present a problem.

Action: Be clear in the report as to the approach taken to score descriptions. We recommend consistency throughout.

Comparing scores

With derived scores to hand, we can now begin to interpret the data and make comparisons within the individual's profile. Before beginning any analysis, it is best to check if it is even sensible to compare a particular set of scores. When tests are co-normed, or standardised in part or in full on the same standardisation group, comparison is facilitated, with publishers providing inter-test comparison tables. However, assessors need to exercise real caution in drawing conclusions from discrepant scores from different tests which, for example, might have been standardised on very different sample populations or at very different times (e.g. 1993 vs. 2013 – a generation apart).

There are some key statistical concepts to consider to help our evaluation of the relevance of observed score differences.

Statistical significance

If the difference between a pair of scores is 'statistically significant', it means that at the chosen level of significance the difference between the scores did not occur by chance: it is not just caused by measurement error. Statistical significance can only be found by reference to test manuals and applies to a pair of scores within a test or between tests which are co-normed. (Note that the concept of statistical significance is quite different from that of confidence intervals, although they are related in that they take the SEm into account.)

Critical values

To identify when a statistically significant difference exists, 'critical values' are published. Tables in test manuals will refer to the minimum difference, in terms of standard scores or scaled scores (at the chosen level of significance), which must exist between the two scores being compared before we can conclude that they are likely to be truly different and not simply caused by measurement error. Once this minimum difference, the 'critical value', is reached or exceeded, the scores can be said to be statistically significantly different from one another.

The choice of which level of significance to work with depends on how certain or confident the assessor would like to be about the score achieved. Levels of significance published generally refer to, for example, the 0.15 or 0.05 levels of significance; this means that the assessor can be respectively 85% confident, or 95% confident, that the difference between the scores does exist. (In the area of statistics, a great deal depends on 'probability' and how confident we would like to be about the conclusions we draw.)

Confidence intervals

Using critical value data is the robust way of establishing statistical significance, and many tests provide this data in their manuals. However, where tests are not co-normed this data is not available, therefore assessors seek alternative approaches to explore differences, although these provide only approximate guidance. One such alternative is to consider the relationship between the confidence intervals around two scores. A score difference can be considered to be worthy of further consideration if the confidence intervals are clear of one another, i.e. they do not overlap.

For example, consider the data below, where the tests are not co-normed:

Test	Score	95% Confidence Interval
Prose reading comprehension	72	64–80
Single-word reading	95	85–105

These confidence intervals do not overlap. As a gap is evident between the upper limit of the comprehension test interval and the lower limit of the single word test interval, we are provided with an indication of an interesting difference, which warrants further consideration and analysis.[4]

However, in a different situation where the confidence intervals do overlap and no such gap is evident, this does not *automatically* imply that the difference should immediately be discounted. It is prudent to consider the individual profile, including the qualitative data, before deciding whether or not a score difference is of interest. This applies most especially in cases where assessors have selected a 95% or above confidence interval, or when the overlap is small.

These decisions about score comparisons will always be accompanied by substantial caution, professional judgement and a requirement to provide sound evidence of any conclusions drawn. This caution applies most especially when tests are not co-normed, as comparisons are not being made across equivalent reference groups. However, this approach using confidence intervals provides a useful starting point from which to reflect on differences. It is an approximate guide rather than a statistical conclusion.

Prevalence rates (also termed 'base rates')

If we have established that a statistically significant difference exists, the next issue is whether or not the difference is diagnostically *meaningful* (rather than just a matter of statistics). There is a great deal of variation of skill within all individuals, and we need to be certain that the differences we are looking at are unusual in comparison to the age-matched population.

Some tests make this easier by providing data about the prevalence of particular score differences. These tell us how frequently such a difference occurred in the standardisation sample and therefore how likely it is to occur to the same degree in the general population. Some test manuals indicate the prevalence rate which is needed for the differences in scores to be of diagnostic interest. However, if we think that perhaps up to 10% of the population might have an SpLD, then

---

[4] It is important to note that even where there are clear gaps between confidence intervals, without critical value data, we still cannot be *certain* the difference is *statistically* significant, and not attributable chance factors.

we might consider that a prevalence rate under 10% becomes diagnostically 'interesting' although not, on its own, 'conclusive'.

Most often, specialist teacher assessors are comparing across tests where there is no formal prevalence data on which to rely. The matter of whether a difference is diagnostically useful must now pass to the assessor. Assessors must use their judgement and experience to decide if a difference is substantial enough to be considered diagnostically interesting. This will draw on underpinning theoretical knowledge as well as the magnitude of the difference. As a useful *starting point* for analysis, the difference will be in the region of 1 to 1.5 standard deviations or more for an unusual difference to be considered possible. This is certainly not a cut-off point, simply an approximate guide.

As a final point in regard to comparing scores, this process should extend to critical evaluation of the overall test battery used. Assessors must be alert to possible over-testing which brings an increasing likelihood of finding one or two unusual scores -- it is always possible to keep testing until one finds a low score! Diagnostic conclusions must rest on *patterns* not individual *scores*.

Professional judgement

If reaching a diagnostic conclusion were simply a matter of comparing scores on statistical grounds, a computer could complete the task easily. It is not, however, and therefore all scores and score differences need the human touch, and throughout the preceding discussion we have placed a great deal of emphasis on the assessor's interpretation.

Assessors must take into account all factors which affect test performance. They must ask if their tests are reliable and valid *in relation to that individual*. The individual's approaches, strategies, and responses to the test situation could all have an impact on the ability of the tests to measure precise skills effectively. Also, assessors must ask if the differences they see could have a substantial impact on performance – either now or in the future, on the activities we have tested or in other areas.

It is not possible to say how many statistical or unusual differences, or of what magnitude, will be needed to confirm a diagnostic conclusion of an SpLD. It could be the case that a number of smaller differences coalesce to create a substantial impact, or one very substantial weakness does the same thing. This is because statistics are, as we said when we began, simply the bones of the story, not the whole. We must add our qualitative data before a full picture can be drawn. From this full picture we must, finally, reflect on underlying theory of SpLDs to support our conclusions.

Action

To structure their investigations, assessors might usefully ask the following set of questions:

- Do test manuals provide sufficient data to confirm statistically significant differences between scores?
- Considering the differences which are statistically significant, how prevalent are they – or, in other words, how frequently do they occur in the standardisation sample, and by extension, in the general population? Are they of sufficient magnitude to be diagnostically useful?
- Are there any differences which, while not statistically confirmed, appear to be of initial interest? In these cases, as there is no prevalence data on which to rely, does my experience suggest this is a difference which could be reliably described as substantial and unusual?
- How does this statistical information fit with the observations, the other qualitative data and underlying theory?

It can be seen that assessors must be observant and perceptive when using statistics, just as much as when using other types of evidence. Test scores, like all other assessment data, must be viewed with skill and judgement in relation to the individual case.

3 Professional Practice

This chapter highlights a range of ethical, legal and professional issues where the application of good practice ensures an assessment is conducted to a high standard. They are just as vital a part of practice as knowledge of theory and testing. As they are substantial topics, the following pages provide an introduction but with additional references for further information.

Ethical, legal and regulatory considerations

Fundamental principles underpin ethical practice when gathering personal data and using diagnostic tests. The Patoss Code of Ethics provides a sound basis for both organisations and individuals to follow regarding professional conduct when carrying out individual assessments. The full code is available on the Patoss website, but some key points are as follows:

- The individual must be firmly placed at the heart of the process: his well-being is the first priority.
- Confidentiality must be maintained at all times and information shared only with the express permission of the individual or, where relevant, his parents/carers. This applies to all information gathered during the process of an assessment, subject to any legal obligations. Particular care must be taken when storing or sending material electronically; check that confidentiality will be maintained by those receiving the material.
- Assessors must work within the limits of their competence. Where presenting problems or the age range fall outside the assessor's area of expertise, the individual should be assisted to find an alternative, appropriately qualified and experienced professional.
- Competence means the ability to offer high quality practice in delivering, interpreting and reporting assessments. This places a responsibility on assessors to ensure that they are up to date with theoretical developments and assessment and teaching practices.
- Before any assessment begins, the purpose and nature of the assessment, how the results will be used and to whom they will be communicated, must be clearly explained to all involved and agreement secured.
- Test materials and resources should be securely stored and their use restricted to those who hold appropriate qualifications.
- Assessors should be properly insured for both legal expenses and any damages that may be awarded should litigation ensue following an assessment. This protects both parties.
- Ethical practice includes adherence to all relevant law. Assessors should be particularly aware of the Equality Act and the Data Protection Act.

The **Equality Act** (2010) makes it unlawful to discriminate against, harass or victimise an individual with a disability. Not all those with an SpLD will be considered to have a disability under the law: it depends on the degree of impact on everyday activity, which is a legal decision. However, in practice, in the same way that diagnostic principles require underlying difficulties to have a marked impact on the individual, most people with SpLDs are likely to be protected by the Act, but the diagnosis itself does not guarantee the legal position.

The Act also places a duty on organisations to anticipate the needs of disabled individuals and to make reasonable adjustments. The Equality and Human Rights Commission produces useful and clear information on the Equality Act, including guidance for schools, FE and HE (www.equalityhumanrights.com).

The **Data Protection Act** (1998) applies to all those who handle personal information. There are individual as well as organisational responsibilities; the Information Commissioner's Office website (www.ico.gov.uk) provides an introduction and updates.

Regulatory and Policy Frameworks: Those working in education need to be aware of the legislative and regulatory framework applying to both mainstream and SEN/disability provision. Updated and comprehensive information for schools is available on the Department for Education website (www.education.gov.uk). As we write, Special Educational Needs and Disability (SEND) is an area of fast-changing Government policy and online resources will be most useful in keeping up to date. Further and Higher Education is currently under the auspices of the Department for Business, Innovation and Skills. Professional networks often provide useful updates.

Examination Access Arrangement Regulations: The Joint Council for Qualifications (JCQ, www.jcq.org.uk) oversees the examination access arrangements for many general and vocational qualifications in the UK. However, while the JCQ scope is wide, it is not universal. Other awarding bodies (for example, those offering specific professional or vocational qualifications) have their own regulations, as do HE institutions and the Scottish qualification authorities. Arrangements for National Curriculum Tests are also different. Familiarity with the relevant, current regulations is important when making recommendations so that individuals are advised correctly about what might be available.

Arrangements do not depend solely on test results, but also on the individual's normal way of working and history of need. Therefore, as final decisions about arrangements rest with examination centres, any assessors working outside schools and colleges must work collaboratively with those institutions to identify and meet individual needs.[1]

---

[1] For fuller discussion of access arrangements, see Jones, A. (Ed.) (2011) *Dyslexia: Assessing the Need for Access Arrangements during Examinations, A Practical Guide*, 4th edition, Patoss.

The SpLD Assessment Standards Committee, the Assessment Practising Certificate and Continuing Professional Development

The SpLD Assessment Standards Committee (SASC www.sasc.org.uk) promotes and supports principles of good practice in diagnostic assessment. All assessors should endeavour to stay up to date with its work. The DfES/SpLD Working Party 2005 report established guidance for assessors in HE and introduced an **approved test list**: SASC regularly updates this guidance. Assessors working in HE must follow this guidance, particularly if the report might be used to support an application for Disabled Students' Allowance, but it has wider application and is considered good practice for all.

The Working Party also instigated the Assessment Practising Certificate scheme. Although at first devised for HE, it is seen as a useful quality standard across all sectors; holders of the APC are given additional recognition by the JCQ, for example. We recommend all specialist teacher assessors gain the certificate. It must be renewed every three years through evidence of diagnostic assessment reporting skills and CPD. The SASC website lists all those whose practising certificates are current and the Patoss website gives full information on the scheme.

CPD is an integral part of professional life and assessors will commit themselves to keeping up-to-date with the ever developing theoretical perspectives as well as issues of practice. In addition to formal courses, participating in local professional networks also makes a valuable contribution.

Working as a sole practitioner

If working independently, particular care is needed to ensure assessments are conducted within a secure framework. In addition to the standard obligations noted above, sole practitioners are likely to need to take extra steps to consider the following areas:

- Insurance – full professional indemnity insurance will be needed, and possibly public liability insurance, depending on circumstances.
- Data protection – independent practitioners are likely to need to register as a 'data controller' and maintain secure records for extended times (see: www.ico.gov.uk).
- Lone working – conduct a risk analysis and take steps to protect yourself and clients.
- Disclosure Baring Service checks (formerly known as Criminal Records Bureau (CRB) checks) – it is advisable to maintain current registration (available through Patoss) and be aware of safeguarding demands for vulnerable children and adults.
- Tax and accounting – HM Revenue and Customs provide clear information on setting up in self-employment (www.hmrc.gov.uk/selfemployed).
- Terms and conditions – it will be helpful to prepare a document setting out terms of work so all parties have clear expectations of the process.

- References – potential clients might value the opportunity to take up references and it is useful to have an up-to-date CV available.
- Record keeping – maintaining accurate, comprehensive and confidential records of all work and communication is necessary.
- Communication with local schools, colleges or universities – established links will allow easier collaboration with professional colleagues when conducting assessments (for example, if background checks need to be made or internal policies confirmed) and are likely to promote a more positive outcome for the pupil or student.
- Professional networks – consider joining professional networks and organisations. Contact with other local assessors will also support CPD and could be very useful for difficult cases or sharing resources.

Summary

- Adherence to a Code of Ethics is imperative for all assessors.
- Maintaining up-to-date knowledge of current legislation, regulations and policy is necessary to understanding the assessment context and to making appropriate recommendations.
- Continuing professional development is a fundamental part of professional practice.

PART TWO

Conducting the Assessment

4 Practical Aspects of Assessment

In this chapter we begin to translate underlying principles into practical action. Subsequent chapters will investigate areas to test and how to interpret results, but first there are the nuts-and-bolts arrangements to be made. They are no less important to a successful outcome.

Prior checks

Before starting to plan the assessment session, do check that an individual assessment is appropriate. Referrals should only be accepted if there is a legitimate reason for the request, if there has been no other assessment recently, and if all parties involved are willing to collaborate in providing essential information and in discussing the findings. If the referral comes from a parent, has the matter first been discussed with the SENCO at the child's school? Importantly, is the individual himself willing to be assessed?

Screening

Sometimes assessors may decide to conduct a screening to inform a decision about whether or not to conduct a full assessment.

Screening tools and methods can take many forms; some are more detailed than others. They range from a yes/no checklist downloadable from the web, to more extensive paper-based or computerised activities available from test publishers. Some must be administered on an individual basis; others are designed for independent or group use. Equally, screening can simply take the form of a structured discussion between a professional and a concerned parent, child or adult to see if the patterns of difficulty described indicate that a diagnostic assessment would be helpful.

The key point about a screening test is that none of the producers of such tests would claim their tests can *diagnose* a difficulty. They provide an *indication* of the difficulties, but might produce either false positives or false negatives. Assessors should choose materials from reputable authors and publishers who clearly identify the rationale and the methods by which conclusions are reached. They should be confident that the tests investigate the target skill and are not inadvertently disadvantaging individuals. For example, complex answer grids can present problems for those with visual-spatial difficulties; computerised tests can disadvantage those without good IT or keyboard skills. Crucially, it must be recognised that a screening tool does not *replace* formal standardised testing where these measures are available.

Some formal screening checklists can nevertheless be useful to incorporate into diagnostic assessments to provide supplementary evidence where formal tests are not available. For example, well-researched checklists in motor coordination and attention are very useful when used knowledgeably; remember, any cut-off points are only guidelines and judgement is needed in interpreting their results.

Assessment planning

Background information

The first stage of the assessment is to gather background information and documentary evidence and this will take time. Many parents will appreciate the opportunity to reflect before answering questions relevant to their child's assessment. Equally, adults will appreciate time to consider their answers. SENCOs, class teachers or other professionals need advance notice to collate any information requested. A full discussion of the information to be collected is part of Chapter 5.

Selecting test materials

The next step is to choose appropriate test materials. Reflect on the purpose of the assessment and the background information gathered. Choose age-appropriate standardised tests and relevant informal additional materials – perhaps curriculum-based assessments such as phonic checklists or subject-related vocabulary. The range of materials used should be broad enough to establish a full profile of skills, strategies and abilities, but without *over*-testing; prioritise as necessary. The aim is to gather enough information to provide a firm platform to make recommendations that meet individual needs.

Planning the pace

Next list all the tests to be used, in order, and note all the materials needed – stopwatch, extra paper, digital recorder, pens and so on – and the key instructions and questions to use. It is a good idea to mix tests that are likely to be stressful, such as reading and spelling, with other activities probably perceived as less difficult, such as vocabulary knowledge or phonological tests. All tests should be delivered in an unhurried manner at a steady pace. Be organised and confident, and practise delivering new tests informally before using them in an assessment.

The overall time needed will vary depending on the age and abilities of the individual, and how attention, mood or cooperation varies across the assessment. A young child will not be able to cope with prolonged testing, whereas more time is often needed with an older, more advanced learner. Plan opportunities for rest breaks or consider breaking the assessment up over more than one day.

However carefully the session is planned, be prepared to be flexible. For example, a learner might read at a level better or worse than expected from the referral information; always have a selection of text passages available to explore reading skills and strategies properly. Alternatively, new information might be uncovered through discussion or observation – perhaps weak expressive vocabulary, poor handwriting, or a significant tendency to inattention, which needs closer investigation through an additional test or checklist. The benefit of having such additional material to hand could make the difference between a clear profile and a confusing one! In complex cases the session might need to be extended or further meetings planned as a result of evidence gained on the day. Do let individuals know at the outset that this is a possibility.

In some cases flexibility might have to extend to re-scheduling the whole session – for example, if the individual is unwell, or suffering significant emotional stress, he is unlikely to perform to the best of his abilities.

The assessment session

Location

Arrange for a quiet, undisturbed location. Consider the age and size of the individual and ensure that the chair and table are at an appropriate relative height, and that lighting is effective without causing glare. Select a seating arrangement which is comfortable for both parties. It should allow easy access to materials for the assessor but keep record papers out of the individual's view – test marks are easily spotted and can be distracting.

Rapport

Good rapport is a crucial part of any assessment. The individual might be very apprehensive and it is important to make sure he is settled and relaxed from the start. He needs to know the purpose of the assessment, what is likely to happen, how long it will take and that he can have a comfort break whenever he needs. Experience and common sense will guide the most effective ways to establish rapport, but allowing this time will immeasurably benefit the overall session and encourage him to give his best efforts in testing.

One potential difficulty in building rapport is that the purpose of the tests is to determine not only what the individual can do, but also the point at which he begins to fail. We need to be able to analyse errors and identify the strategies he is using. The progressive difficulty of tests should be explained. For example, with a primary age child, one could say: *'I use this test with much older students so it will become difficult and I don't expect you to get it all right.'* With older individuals, explain the need to see where the difficulties lie in order to plan the way forward.

Throughout the assessment give appropriate praise and encourage continued effort. However, do not be tempted to give feedback as to whether responses were right or wrong, but try to respond with a neutral phrase such as *'Thank you'*, or *'You are working hard'*. For older pupils and adults, an explanation at the outset that this kind of feedback cannot be given might be of help.

Overall, assessment has the potential to be a stressful occasion, but by building a good relationship with the individual the assessor can instead create a positive experience.

Administering tests

Good preparation will enable the assessor to deliver tests confidently and move smoothly between activities, noting if the learner appears to need a break. When administering standardised tests, it is vital to follow the detailed instructions in the manual. Each test is standardised using these procedures, so deviating from them will invalidate results. If necessary, explain that a script has to be followed.

If an individual becomes distressed by his 'failures', it is legitimate in these circumstances to discontinue testing before the test's stated cut-off point is reached. However, in this case, a standardised score cannot be calculated and the reason should be explained in the report.

Open questions

When exploring strategies or difficulties it is important to use open questions – avoiding closed questions that would encourage just a yes/no response. For example, *'Do you find reading difficult?'* will provide little information, but *'Tell me about how you find reading'* is more akin to the beginning of a story. This approach has the benefit of allowing the individual to choose his own priorities rather than the assessor inadvertently controlling the response or suggesting difficulties.

Recording

It is vital to keep a written record of responses to activities, including detailed notes of behaviour during tests, as well as other observations and discussions. The way an activity is tackled is as important as the outcome in both standardised tests and informal tasks – for example, the same score might be achieved with ease or with significant effort – so reliance on memory is not recommended. Perhaps explain *'I need to make notes to help me remember what you have done when I write my report.'*

Do ensure test record forms and all working papers are retained in the case file.

An audio recording of some parts or all of the assessment might also be useful, especially to support accurate marking – some test items require very fast or very precise recording of responses. Check that this is acceptable to the individual and make the process unobtrusive. A small digital recorder placed discreetly on the desk will soon be forgotten. Indexing the recording will make it easier and faster to retrieve the information later.

Feedback and discussion

At the end of the session discuss how the assessment went, making a point of highlighting any areas of strength or competence noted. Ask the individual how he feels and acknowledge his cooperation during the session. Many individuals will want to know what the main impressions are straight away. Be honest about what is immediately obvious, but explain that time is needed to analyse all the results carefully and think things through. Explain when the report will be available and what opportunity will be available to discuss its implications. Older pupils and adults might appreciate an invitation to bring someone with them to any meeting to discuss feedback.

Summary

- Prepare assessment materials carefully in the light of the background information. However, be flexible and ready to respond to new evidence as it emerges.
- Allow time to establish rapport with the child or adult. This is crucial.
- Make notes on the individual's responses in each assessment activity and his reactions during the session.
- The aim of the assessment is to gather enough information about the individual's abilities and skills in order to plan effective ways forward, without over-testing.

Treat the individual as an active and equal partner during the assessment session as well as in subsequent discussions about the results and their implications for the future. Providing useful, accessible feedback is an integral part of the assessment.

5 Main Areas of Investigation

We are now in a position to begin to tackle the assessment itself, and in this chapter we work through the main areas we need to explore. Our aim is to tease out what the child or adult can and cannot do and the reasons why he is finding particular tasks difficult. We might have a hypothesis that an SpLD is present, but we should always keep an open mind and take an approach which reflects on the emerging evidence, rather than one that seeks support for a predetermined view.

We will use a set of core formal tests, some informal measures and also have to hand further materials to respond to issues and questions that emerge as we work with the individual. Throughout, two things will be equally vital: accurate test marking and close investigation of *how* the assessment is tackled. Close observation, note of strategies used and sensitive questioning will add richness to the test scores and provide supplementary evidence contributing to our conclusion beyond the numerical data.

We will consider each area of testing in turn – cognitive abilities, attainments and additional aspects. However, we begin with the step which helps both to plan the assessment and inform the outcomes – the background information. Even before beginning this step, it is good practice to have been in contact with and spoken to the child or adult; it is reassuring and allows the necessary arrangements to be made.

Background information

Background information is fundamental to an accurate assessment. There are three reasons for this. It allows us to:
- place the assessment data in context;
- eliminate other possible explanations for the current difficulties;
- explore the history of difficulties and any typical patterns of SpLD, especially in those areas less easily exposed by formal testing – those manifestations of SpLDs we talked about in Chapter 1.

In exploring the background information, there are fundamental areas to cover, but the detail and depth of each will vary with age and context. Assessors can build their own questions, drawing on the categories below, expanding or minimising elements as necessary.

Medical and developmental history

This must include checking on vision and hearing history as well as establishing that no health or significant medical factors could have influenced learning. It will also include checks on speech and language development and initial questions about fine and gross motor skills. For children, in particular, there will be questions about early developmental milestones in physical and language development. Ask too about any history of language/literacy difficulties or known history of specific learning difficulties in the family.

Language learning environment

Before beginning, we will need to be sure the individual has had adequate opportunity to develop spoken language skills. Is English the first language? What language is spoken at home? If English is an additional language, questions about the early acquisition of literacy skills in the first language will be needed.

Educational factors

It is vital to ask about early learning experience. Were reading, spelling, writing and maths skills gained easily or with difficulty? A comprehensive history of education is also needed. Assessors will endeavour to establish if teaching has been consistent and suitable, and the nature and success of any previous assessments or learning support, as well as academic progress and achievements to date.

Social and affective factors

Here we wish to investigate broadly but not intrusively and consider if social, family or home circumstances have had a significant impact on learning. For example, questions about whether school is enjoyable, the favourite (and least favourite) topics and subjects, and friendships in school might be relevant. The adult might also have interesting stories to tell here.

Also, some insight into levels of confidence, motivation to learn, temperament and so on will inform our picture of the wider influences on learning. This might extend to questions relating to anxiety and emotional well-being, and possibly mental health, as these too can impact significantly on assessment performance.

Current difficulties, interests and aspirations

Of course we need to establish the reason for the assessment and the current problems, but it is also important to learn about the person – his interests, hobbies, and enthusiasms as well as his priorities for learning and moving forwards. What are his hopes and aspirations? Ask too about how he perceives his strengths. All individuals, even young children, can contribute to this process, which will help the assessor create individual and relevant recommendations.

Gathering the information

We have considered the categories of information, but assessors must also decide *how* to collect it. The main sources will be home, school or college and the individual himself. Contact with parents, teachers and other professionals will vary depending on the individual's age.

The methods to collect information vary too and assessors will choose those which suit the circumstances. Well-designed pre-assessment questionnaires are very useful and they also guide the choice of test materials. Assessors might need to speak directly to some parties involved. A structured interview schedule will also ensure that all relevant ground is covered during the session.

In designing questionnaires and conducting interviews, remember always to use open-ended questions, so the question itself does not prompt the response – for example, ask *'What are you finding difficult at school?'* rather than *'Do you find French or revision difficult?'*

Home

Parents or carers of primary or secondary pupils are usually the best source of detail about early development and school experience. They will understand their child's temperament and interests and be able to comment on any family history of learning difficulties.

They might also be able to provide information about coping strategies and problems not seen at school. To give just two examples, the pupil may appear well organised at school, but it may be the support at home which makes this possible. Or, behaviour problems might emerge at home as the stress and effort of coping all day at school results in tiredness and irritability in the evening.

Do ask to see copies of school reports or earlier assessments by other professionals, and remember to check for details such as the date of birth, contact details, the school year, the stage of education, educational qualifications, etc.

School/College

A brief questionnaire might be constructed for the school or college. In a primary school, the child's current class teacher will be an important source of information, whereas in a secondary school or college, views of key staff members will be needed, perhaps gathered via the SENCO. Questions about performance in relation to effort, spoken communication in relation to written expression, attention and concentration will be useful, as well as literacy and educational measures. There might also be IEPs or screening/group test results available and examples of work can also be collected.

The individual

Children and adults should be encouraged to participate as fully as possible in the assessment process and all ages will often welcome the opportunity to give their views about their learning experiences. This is particularly the case for older pupils and adults who have not had a chance to discuss their difficulties in any detail before. Of course, some might be reluctant, so sensitive questioning which explains why the information is needed is required.

Cognitive abilities

Cognitive underlying ability

Individually administered tests of underlying verbal and non-verbal ability will be included in the battery. They contribute to our understanding of the overall cognitive profile and help plan a differentiated teaching programme. Although group tests are available, many are designed for screening and provide only brief measures. Also, they generally involve reading and writing and offer limited opportunity for observation and are therefore not so useful.

Verbal ability

Verbal ability measures help us understand the individual's capabilities with spoken language. As we will also look at written language skills, which quite possibly prompted the referral, we can then compare the two. Verbal abilities are often investigated as follows:

Verbal Ability		
Vocabulary knowledge	Receptive / Expressive Language	
	This measures the individual's ability to explain the meaning of increasingly complex words out of context. It tests the ability both to understand the word and to express that understanding.	
	Receptive Language	
	This type of test measures the understanding of spoken words, often by reference to a picture. It has a key benefit in that it does not ask the individual to explain his understanding.	
Verbal reasoning ability	This test asks the individual to understand and identify links and relationships between words and/or verbal concepts. Sometimes a test contains a general knowledge element and assessors should note if this component prevents the individual reaching higher levels.	

A choice might be made between a receptive language test, or one which also tests expressive language – but in some cases both are needed. As a rule, assessors might begin with a test containing expressive language, but it is very helpful to have a receptive vocabulary test available. For example, if a test including *expressive* vocabulary does not seem to capture the full extent of the individual's knowledge, the *receptive* vocabulary might provide a more reliable measure. Or a receptive vocabulary test might be more appropriate for a very young learner or a reluctant pupil or adult. Comparisons between expressive and receptive language can be illuminating as to the source of any difficulty.

As well as conducting formal tests, observe *spoken* language skills. Note the quality and fluency of language used, as at any age there may be strengths which are not apparent in test scores.

Non-verbal ability

Tests of non-verbal ability explore a person's ability to reason beyond the ability to use language, providing an alternative and additional view of aptitude for learning. They investigate logical thinking and problem-solving skills and the aptitude for learning through direct experience, normally under timed conditions. Again individually administered tests are best.

Non-Verbal Ability	
Non-verbal ability tests assess visual perception, the ability to perceive and understand what is seen.	
Visual reasoning ability	Such tests assess the ability to analyse and interpret information presented in a visual format. Tests are most often in the form of a Matrices task.
Visual-spatial ability	This measures the ability to understand and interpret what is seen, often using practical construction tasks, for example, reproducing abstract designs using puzzle chips, or blocks.

Observation of performance will be needed to evaluate the result, especially if there are marked differences between the different types of skill. Was there a difficulty with distinguishing colour, understanding a grid format, physically manipulating three-dimensional pieces, or a problem with the timed element?

Cognitive abilities: verbal short-term and working memory

Investigation into verbal memory needs to be as thorough as possible, as we know that it is fundamental in the learning processes. It is also a key to performance in a very wide range of tasks and activities.

Verbal Memory	
Verbal short-term memory	These tests assess the ability to hold onto and simply repeat information stored in our minds for a brief time.
Verbal working memory	In contrast, working memory tests investigate the ability to both store and then manipulate information.

These skills are tested in various guises, often including repetition and/or manipulation of strings of numbers, letters or words. As always, the assessor should note any strategies being used during the tests – for example, verbal rehearsal or creating visual images – to evaluate the validity of the result.

Informal measures and observations of working memory are also very helpful. The assessor might include a dictation, a note-taking, or a listening comprehension task. Of course these activities are not pure tests of working memory, but useful observations can be drawn from them.

Visual memory

Reflecting models of memory, tests of visual memory might also be included. They will give useful information about particular strengths and weaknesses, and can contribute to patterns perhaps seen elsewhere in verbal and visual domains.

Cognitive abilities: phonological awareness

Tests of *phonological awareness* assess the ability to identify sounds in spoken words as well as the ability to manipulate these sounds – a crucial skill in literacy development.

These tests form part of the core assessment battery, but the depth of testing will vary. For younger pupils more detail is needed to support teaching, but adults with very weak literacy skills might also need to know where they are in their phonological development, for the same purpose. Older pupils and well-taught or well-compensated individuals will need more challenging tasks. In every case the assessor should note if timed conditions affect results – it might be the speed element that is weak, rather than the awareness. It is important that these tests involve no written material.

We set out below the increasingly challenging steps in testing. Consider the stages of phonological development and the age of the individual to decide where to begin. Formal tests will be used where available, although supplementary informal tasks are often immensely valuable.

Syllable knowledge

Are checks needed on the awareness of syllables? Can the individual identify the number of beats there are in words of varying length, perhaps by simultaneously tapping or clapping the syllables whilst saying the word?

Segmentation skills – rhyme and alliteration

Can the individual differentiate between parts of words? Segmentation is classically assessed using alliteration and rhyme judgement tests. Those for younger pupils often include pictures of the words.

Phonemic awareness

Now we investigate the ability to manipulate phonemes. Alliteration requires identification of initial phonemes, but further investigation might be needed. Deletion of phonemes is a more demanding task and can target middle and end sounds. Can the individual repeat words and then again with certain phonemes deleted? For example, 'Say might *but without the /t/.*' It is important to give the instructions using the *sound* of the letter to be deleted, not the name.

Spoonerisms

A spoonerism requires the transposition of the initial phonemes of two words: for example, the individual presented with *car park* must respond *par cark*. It is more challenging than the task above as it involves both phonological awareness and working memory. Might this be an interesting task for the well-compensated or older student? There are formal tests of spoonerisms available, or an informal assessment can be constructed.

Spoken language

Further insight into phonological awareness can be gained through observation of spoken language. There might be errors in speech, or mumbled and/or mispronounced (especially multi-syllable) words, malapropisms (where similar sounding words are confused, for example specific/pacific), and so forth, as well as words being used incorrectly. Older individuals will often report this frustrating tendency and parents/teachers will observe it in younger pupils.

Cognitive abilities: speed of processing

Speed of Processing	
Phonological processing speed	This investigates how quickly language can be retrieved and articulated.
Visual processing speed	By contrast, this tests how quickly an individual can work with visual information.

Phonological processing speed is often measured by a rapid-naming task: individuals are asked to label, for example, numbers, letters, objects or colours, in timed conditions. These tasks are designed to expose weaknesses in working at speed with verbal information – bringing well-known information quickly to mind – a vital skill in reading and writing tasks.

Visual processing speed assesses how quickly an individual can process and organise visual information. These are rarely 'pure' tests. They are often copying tasks using unfamiliar symbols, also demanding visual tracking, visual short-term memory, hand-eye coordination, fine motor control, attention and concentration. Sometimes it is possible to note if one aspect is more difficult than another. If the test allows for a parallel oral version of the writing task, the results can be usefully compared.

Attainments

Reading

The key areas of accuracy, comprehension, fluency and speed must all be explored. With tests carefully chosen to suit the individual, each one can be used diagnostically, not simply to gather a score. What we need is detail about the strategies used at word and text level to understand the individual's skills.

To gain accurate detail, many assessors find it helpful to audio record the reading so they can replay it if necessary when marking.

Considering visual stress

Before beginning these investigations, do check if there are any visual distortions when reading (see later in this chapter for more detail). If a problem is reported, the assessor might offer a choice of coloured overlays for the individual to trial with an informal reading task. If a positive benefit is noted, assessors could allow the use of the overlay in the reading tests to remove the influence of visual stress from the results, therefore gaining a more reliable measure of underlying reading skill. However, note this in the report and take comparative measures without the overlay if necessary. If assessors conclude that the visual stress is so significant that it will undermine test results, further professional referral should be made before continuing the assessment.

Book knowledge

With a young child, 'book knowledge' should be checked at the outset. Does he know the front and back of a book; the difference between a line and a sentence; etc? It is important to establish if the child has sufficient knowledge of the *language of literacy* to benefit fully from the teaching.

Sound-symbol correspondence

Can the individual read and write both the *name* and the *sound* of each letter of the alphabet with confidence? Is there an awareness of the difference between vowels and consonants? For older pupils and adults, assessors can decide if this exploration is needed after initial observations of reading and writing skill, as they might already have demonstrated good skills in these areas.

Single-word reading

A standardised single-word reading test will assess sight-word knowledge and decoding skills without the clues of context and grammar. It establishes quickly a reading level to inform later testing, and begins to uncover reading strategies.

We need to know where and why reading accuracy breaks down so that appropriate recommendations can be made. Careful observation will tell us the relative success of sound-based or visual strategies (perhaps working out words by analogy to other known words or familiar word components), and how (or if) he tackles unfamiliar words.

It is good to begin with an untimed test or one with a generous time allowance, to find out what the reader can do with plenty of time. Depending on success, a timed test can then follow to understand how automatically the individual can recognise words, although it is good to include this in most assessments since working at speed becomes important as demands increase.

In addition, graded word reading tests or subject-specific word tests might be used. Graded tests, found in many phonically-based teaching schemes, can be especially useful for younger and weaker readers, as the systematic checking establishes a suitable starting point for instruction. For older pupils and adults, vocabulary relevant to a course or work environment might also be needed. An adult working in catering might need to be able to read a range of vocabulary based on menus such as *gateaux* or *spaghetti*. There are published lists of essential subject vocabulary or they can often be obtained beforehand from the relevant teacher or tutor.

Non-word reading

Non-word reading tests tell us about the ability to use phonemic decoding skills and therefore the ability to read unfamiliar words. Both timed and untimed tests are useful. A timed test adds a demand for efficiency as well as accuracy, providing further information.

Reading comprehension

A good reader is able to combine seamlessly a range of skills: general language knowledge, context, word prediction, whole-word recognition, phonemic decoding and the ability to switch strategies according to the difficulty of the material. However, if someone clearly struggles at early levels with single-word reading, while his ability to read a text could be tested informally at an easy level, it might instead be appropriate to investigate his ability to understand whole text in a *listening* comprehension task.

Oral reading comprehension

It is very useful to hear the individual read a text aloud to gather more information about his reading strategies. It can be timed to measure speed, and the ability to read prose with appropriate expression and fluency can be observed.

Points to note:

- Does he read fluently or are there hesitations? How does he tackle individual words?
- Does he make appropriate use of punctuation?
- Is he able to self-correct accuracy errors using context?
- Is he able to monitor meaning as he reads?
- Is he able to comprehend text better when reading aloud, or when reading silently?
- Is he able to hold onto and recall the information he has read?

A careful running record of the reading will be needed, noting errors and test behaviour (see page 173 for a detailed guide to miscue analysis).

Silent reading comprehension

These tests more closely reflect the real demands of reading in the classroom, in study and everyday activity and are particularly useful from secondary age and beyond. Some tests include a measure of silent reading speed, but if not, it is better to explore the silent reading speed separately from the reading comprehension text, so as not to interfere with the individual's preferred way of tackling text. One approach is to time an informal, short, silent reading task, followed by brief questions about the content, and then calculate the words per minute rate to compare with the oral reading speed.

Considering the different methods tests use to measure reading skills will help interpretation. For example, if comprehension is tested after the text is read aloud, this can disadvantage the person with dyslexia, as attention and effort are taken up by the demands of decoding, leaving little room for any useful monitoring of meaning. Other tests do not allow the reader to refer back to the text to answer questions, placing greater demands on working memory.

Beyond formal tests, a range of texts could be used to explore reading. An assessor's reading 'kit', therefore, could usefully include passages from reading books, curriculum texts, newspapers or magazines, appropriate for a range of ages, ability levels and interests.

Listening comprehension

A listening comprehension task will tell us more about the individual's ability to understand and gain meaning from a text where there is no demand on decoding. It can be a useful additional measure, particularly where there are concerns about reading comprehension, so the two ways of accessing information can be compared. Formal tests of listening comprehension are available, or else a passage from one of the parallel forms of the prose reading tests might be used informally.

Spelling

Begin the analysis of spelling skills with a standardised single-word test. Spelling is nearly always a deep-rooted and persistent problem for those with dyslexia and this area must be treated sensitively. Assessors might encourage individuals to 'have a go' at words they are not sure of, as this will throw additional light on where difficulties lie.

A careful analysis of errors will tell us whether the individual is using sound-based or visual strategies and where he is on the stage of development. Where assessment results will be used to establish a baseline for teaching, it might be necessary to supplement the formal assessment, perhaps by using high-frequency words from key stage lists or relevant subject-specific vocabulary.

Free writing

Free writing is an opportunity for the individual to express his ideas, interests, or awareness of the world and he should be encouraged in his efforts. The aim of the task is to investigate a wide range of skills, and assessors will consider the following core areas:

- quality and creativity of ideas and content – is there any discrepancy between the ability to talk about a subject and write about it?

- extent of vocabulary; use of language; clarity and fluency of expression – again, is there any contrast between written and spoken skill?
- organisation of thoughts;
- structure, at sentence and overall text level;
- accuracy in relation to grammar and punctuation;
- spelling in context, identifying any contrasts with single-word skills;
- letter formation, size, spacing, positioning, and pencil grip;
- handwriting in relation to legibility, fluency and speed.

When working with children, the assessor will normally be in contact with the child's teacher(s) and it can be very useful to see examples of unaided and uncorrected free writing produced in the classroom – perhaps first drafts of writing, or from planning and 'rough' books. However, it is still important to observe the process of writing at first hand, even if the writing is effortful and the piece is brief. Offer support if it is requested – for example, where to begin, or with the spelling of words – but make a note of this.

Except for the very young, a measure of writing speed is needed, but it is complex, as it depends not only on motor skills, but on fluency of thought and the ability to translate ideas into words. There are other variables too – for example, a lack of confidence in spelling might interfere with writing fluency. Copying and/or dictation tasks can help to tease these strands apart, as they remove the need to be creative. The speed of handwriting can then be compared to the writing speed in the compositional task.

Numeracy

Unexpected weaknesses in mathematics can be part of several SpLD profiles, although for some this area will not be a priority and for others maths will be an area of strength. Judge where to begin the assessment and how extensively to investigate, using knowledge of the mathematical skills expected for the individual's age and stage of development and information on current skill levels.

Areas to assess might include:
- number sense, counting (both forwards and backwards, in ones, or in multiples), the ability to read and write numbers, awareness of place value, and estimating skills;
- knowledge of number bonds and multiplication tables, and investigation of the ease with which these number facts can be retrieved;
- basic mathematical operations of addition, subtraction, multiplication and division at a level appropriate to the individual;
- recognition of symbols and knowledge and understanding of the language of numeracy;
- confidence in everyday numeracy tasks – time, money, measures, etc;
- current curriculum or work-related tasks;
- maths anxiety – this can be a key reason for difficulty, therefore use of a structured questionnaire will be helpful to explore this area.

Assessors should be ready to use concrete materials where needed – for example, counters and money to explore understanding of basic number concepts – and visual representation in other cases, fractions for example.

A standardised test of arithmetic might be a useful place to start – although this can be very daunting indeed. A further standardised test of mathematical reasoning and problem solving will also be helpful to understand fully the current situation – one which goes beyond arithmetic and includes word problems, use of data, charts and graphs, and everyday measures, for example.

Throughout, note unobtrusively how problems are tackled, then, at the end of the test, ask the individual to describe his methods of working in a few key areas. This will show where the process is breaking down, or highlight some ingenious strategies and strengths, even if basic arithmetic is weak.

Where a detailed understanding is needed or if a formal test is inappropriate, perhaps for the very young or the very nervous, an informal approach will be more useful. This could involve sets of questions to be solved or graded into a 'can do / might be able to do / cannot do yet' categorising system. This can be an excellent way to begin a conversation with an individual of any age about their maths skills.

Further assessment areas

The tests above represent the core areas to be investigated, but as evidence emerges, it might be necessary to probe more deeply in certain areas. We discuss the most common of these now.

Motor coordination

The background information and test performance might prompt an assessor to explore motor coordination more fully – this is often needed to understand the profile accurately.

Open-ended questions should be asked about whether there are, or were in the past, any difficulties with gross motor skills and motor coordination. Investigate difficulties with balance, posture and physical activity. Screening checklists for dyspraxia are available.

With young children, the focus will be on the learning of early physical activities – for example, crawling, feeding, talking, dressing, using utensils, tying shoelaces and so on – exploring any difficulties in these areas. With older pupils and adults, include questions around learning to ride a bicycle, or swim, playing sports and team games, learning to drive, bumping into things or people, carrying trays of glasses, and so on. Some caution is needed, as adults might have compensated for these types of difficulty, practised hard on a particular skill, or simply now avoid them.

Motor coordination skills should also be explored at the fine motor level by looking at any difficulties experienced with handwriting, typing, or playing a musical instrument, for example.

Visual-motor integration and visual perception

Successfully integrating visual and motor skills and accurately perceiving and interpreting detailed visual information are necessary for many tasks – not least reading and writing! Difficulties here are often associated with poor motor coordination, and separate investigation of these strands will identify if one – or more – of these aspects is a notable feature of the profile. Comparing these results with tests of copying speed, handwriting speed and tests of hand-eye coordination is useful.

Visual stress

We have noted that assessors should consider early in an assessment if an individual suffers from visual disturbance when looking at print. This problem might manifest in a number of ways, for example:

- difficulties with tracking lines of print;
- skipping or repeating lines when reading, or omitting words;
- using a finger to point to words or complaining of print moving, or merging;
- suffering from excessive fatigue, or showing signs of squinting or repetitive blinking;
- difficulty with near- or far-point copying; resting head on the desk whilst writing or reading; occluding one eye;
- untidy presentation of written work, or writing inconsistently placed on the page, perhaps moving away from the margin.

Attention and concentration

Difficulties with attention and concentration are common across the range of specific learning difficulties. However, if the background information indicates that these difficulties appear substantial and pervasive, they will need further investigation. Unless the assessor has received training in this area, the investigation will require a referral to another professional who has knowledge and experience of this complex condition. As well as the normal range of tests, this assessor would explore important areas such as: attention control and the ability to vary attention as required, impulsivity and the ability to inhibit response, motivation, procrastination, day-dreaming, organisation and memory. There are recognised ratings scales available. Depending on the outcome, a further referral to a medical practitioner may be necessary (see Chapters 1 and 7).

English as an Additional Language (EAL)

Where English is an Additional Language, there are a number of factors and cautions beyond all those already mentioned to take into account when selecting assessment materials. The assessor should evaluate these issues and ask herself if she has sufficient knowledge to conduct the assessment, and if not to say so.

Firstly, it is important to check that the individual has sufficient fluency in English for a diagnostic assessment to be carried out at all. If questions or instructions are not fully understood, results will of course be unreliable.

If spoken language skills are considered sufficient for an assessment, but not fully fluent, a balance must be struck between maintaining the test standardisation and adapting the administration so that the individual understands the task. If instructions are significantly varied, it might not be appropriate to use standardised scores at all, but to use tests diagnostically. Most of the tests used are normed on those whose first language is English, so questions must be asked about the usefulness of the comparative data. On the other hand, it may be possible to select tests with EAL cohort data.

Secondly, the individual's linguistic and cultural background must be considered carefully. Some tests have a cultural bias – verbal ability tests and reading tests, in particular – so results might not be considered as diagnostically useful. Also, the sound structure of the first language might have an effect on tests drawing on phonological skills and be seen in reading and spelling results. In addition, the written structure of the language might be very different and influence how the new language is constructed. Therefore some research into the individual's first language will be extremely valuable.

Having reflected on these issues, assessors can plan a suitable test battery. In addition to standard practice, the following might also be included:

- a receptive language test – this will be particularly useful;
- phonological awareness using non-words, rather than real English words;
- rapid-naming tests used informally in the first language, giving an indication of the speed and fluency of language retrieval when compared to the results gained when tested in English;
- reading speed in English and the first language;
- culturally relevant qualitative reading/writing tasks;
- free writing tasks in both English and the first language. 'Google' or 'Bing' translation facilities might provide some support.
- In tests of literacy, the *type* of errors can be carefully analysed.

As usual, the investigation will include the strategies used to carry out a task. Particularly note if the individual translates from English into the first language for processing and then back into English again before responding, as this clearly imposes an additional load.

The next step

There has been much to investigate! By now, the assessor is in a privileged position, holding onto a great deal of information gathered from a wide range of sources. The next task is to draw it together into a coherent whole. This is where the knowledge and skill of the assessor become paramount, as of course it is vital that all the evidence is sifted and interpreted in an accurate way.

6 Interpreting the Evidence: Scores, Observations and Comparisons

Our task as assessors might now be compared to assembling a jigsaw puzzle. We take each single piece of data, evaluate it, and consider where it fits with the other pieces until an overall picture becomes clear. This is not always a straightforward task; individuals are of course all different, so we can expect to see many different patterns emerge.

The first step to solving the puzzle and accurately interpreting the data is to reflect on the results of each test in turn. There is much more to do than just calculate the test score – although do check before starting an analysis that scores have been calculated correctly. Many a strange profile can be explained by a marking error! As we cannot present and interpret every potential test result, in the first part of this chapter we discuss useful questions and the common themes that emerge from the answers. These will help assessors consider what the score and the qualitative data might reveal, while being ever mindful that individual circumstances will apply, further questions might be raised and alternative interpretations required.

The second step is to take a wide view of the picture that emerges and decide which diagnostic label best represents the dominant features seen. In the next chapter we provide some typical profiles which assessors can use, *alongside theoretical definitions*, to help arrive at the diagnostic conclusion. We know individuals rarely fit into neat boxes, but we can aim to find a supportive 'description of best fit' to help them understand their difficulties.

We need to begin our evaluation by asking the following questions:

- Is the *score* a true reflection of the individual's skills in this area? Are there any influences on the scores to consider?
- *How* did the individual achieve this result – what methods and strategies did he use? This information will support both diagnostic outcomes and recommendations.
- Can this score be usefully compared with others? Why? What does that reveal?

Such questions will lead to a full picture drawing on all that was found in the assessment; it is what sets an *assessor* apart from a *test administrator* and can make the difference between a superficial testing session and a supportive and informative assessment.

Verbal abilities

Strengths in underlying verbal ability support success in school, college and work, and are an important indicator of potential. Even so, we would never want to use this data as our *only* guide to potential – many factors play a part in achieving success, such as levels of motivation, opportunities available, the quality of teaching, training and experience.

Verbal abilities can be an area of strength for those with SpLDs. One characteristic of dyslexia, for example, is that spoken language knowledge is often stronger than written language skill. However, if weaknesses emerge, understanding their nature, whether related to SpLD or not, will help inform recommendations.

Weak scores can of course simply mean verbal ability is indeed weak: the individual has difficulty with acquiring vocabulary and lacks word knowledge. Background information might help to explain this. Perhaps there was a lack of exposure to a rich language environment? Perhaps the score is less useful as a measure of ability because English is not the first or dominant language? Also, given that verbal ability tends to be developed in formal schooling and that tests tend to have a cultural bias, are these issues a factor in the low score?

Yet verbal ability measures can also be weak for reasons related to specific difficulties. As a general point, we know that reading experience is a major route to acquiring language skills. If this experience is lacking due to an SpLD, opportunities to develop language knowledge might have been limited. Looking in greater detail at test performance might illuminate other potential reasons for weak scores.

Points to consider

In receptive/expressive verbal ability tests (vocabulary and verbal reasoning)

- Did the individual produce precise and confident definitions of words? Could he easily see the relationships between words?

Or

- Did he have difficulty in *finding* or *retrieving* the words, even when it appeared he knew them, affecting his ability to articulate his knowledge clearly?
- Did he work quickly and fluently, or slowly and in an effortful way?
- Were there difficulties in *organising* words for effective expression? Was it apparent that while he understood the word or verbal relationship, he could not effectively express his understanding *succinctly*? Did this mean he worked in a circuitous or repetitive way, missing the central point?

■ Did the test design restrict his success? For example, did a lack of general knowledge, rather than reasoning or language ability, influence the result? If the assessor feels this had a notable impact, the report might suggest the score could be something of an underestimate – were stronger expressive skills observed in the assessment session or good verbal skills noted by teachers?

These questions begin to explore *how* the score was achieved. Organisational or retrieval problems might provide an initial indicator of a specific difficulty with the processing of language. Alternatively, the key difficulty noted might be speed of working – the individual could complete the task accurately but not quickly. Difficulties with speed are common across SpLD profiles, so are always of interest. Consider how this would have an impact in daily life in oral and written activities. For example, if it is hard to retrieve words in speech, it is hard to retrieve words for writing. Look to see if the range of vocabulary used in writing is more restricted than expected.

In receptive vocabulary tests
■ Were there any differences between receptive and expressive language skills?
■ Was there any difficulty with managing the visual detail in the test pictures?

A significant contrast between receptive and expressive skills might be found. For those with some specific difficulties, it can be easier to demonstrate understanding by linking a concept to a picture rather than having to find and articulate words to express the understanding – especially where very precise answers are needed to gain marks in tests. Perhaps the receptive test demonstrated greater understanding of language than is observed. Might teachers have been underestimating the individual's ability because of poor spoken contributions in class?

If expressive and/or receptive verbal abilities are very weak in combination with poor construction of oral and written language, might the problem be a specific language impairment requiring referral to a speech and language specialist? Look much more widely for information to support this hypothesis – to reading comprehension, to social language use, to phonology and use of grammar and to evidence beyond the assessment session.

Non-verbal abilities

In contrast to verbal abilities, non-verbal abilities are not as dependent on formal education. They develop through more general, practical-type learning situations and are less influenced by environmental factors. However, occasionally, if a child or adult has not been exposed to puzzles, for example, he might not do as well in tasks which include these activities.

Again, many with SpLDs will have strengths in their non-verbal abilities. Good scores show abilities in analysing and interpreting visual information, applying logical reasoning skills to solve problems, and paying attention to visual detail when organising information. Weak scores show relative inabilities to work in this domain, but they *might* also highlight subtle signs of a specific difficulty. Interesting contrasts might emerge between different types of non-verbal tasks. If so, what *type* of activity was more difficult?

Points to consider

■ Did a timing element affect the results? Could the individual work accurately but not at speed? If he was allowed to continue after the test's formal cut-off point, could he solve items at more advanced levels with additional time? This information could be used as informal evidence of ability without time pressure.

■ Did the individual use any strategies to support problem solving, such as talking through his approach, using language to support the visual task? If so, could he be advised to use this strategy in the recommendations to support learning?

■ Might working memory ability have interfered with the performance?

In matrices-type tasks

■ Were test items visually confusing or too 'busy'? Any problems with colour? Any effects of visual stress?

In practical construction-type tasks

■ Were the small pieces hard to manipulate and control? Was there a lack of confidence in moving the pieces and 'having a go'? Was it easy or difficult to manage the switch between 2D and 3D work?

If weaknesses in particular areas emerge (perhaps in speed or working memory), or use of strategies is observed, it is helpful to consider if they are mirrored by evidence in other tests, for example in literacy tests.

Specific issues with speed, visual accuracy and/or motor coordination can be characteristic of SpLD profiles and these weaknesses might be reflected in lower non-verbal ability scores. Very low results in visual-spatial tasks alongside evidence of motor coordination difficulties could indicate a need to refer to a physiotherapist or an occupational therapist. This combination might lead assessors to consider if dyspraxia is part of the picture, but again a wider view of the cognitive and attainment profile, as well as background, will be needed before reaching that conclusion. Other SpLDs also tend to show relative weaknesses in non-verbal ability patterns – dyscalculia, for example.

Considering contrasts between verbal and non-verbal scores

A significant *discrepancy* between verbal and non-verbal abilities is of interest in relation to learning styles and planning programmes of support. Some individuals prefer to work in a kinaesthetic way and they find learning 'by doing', by direct experience and using a logical approach, very much easier than learning through language. On the other hand, some find they rely on words and language to learn.

Discrepancies between these two domains of underlying ability are not a diagnostic requirement for any SpLD – individuals might show unusual discrepancies or they might find their abilities are broadly equal.

Those who have substantial, well-below-average difficulties across both verbal and non-verbal domains are likely to have a range of special educational needs and referral to other professionals might be necessary.

Overall, information about underlying abilities is best used to inform knowledge of approaches to learning. However, verbal and non-verbal measures also have a very useful contribution to make as reference points when considering whether unusual contrasts exist in the rest of the cognitive profile. They are not the only reference points, but they are useful ones.

Verbal short-term and working memory

In profiles of dyslexia, a characteristic pattern is for scores in verbal short-term and working memory to be weak and substantially lower than the scores in tests of verbal and non-verbal ability. Yet we need to consider how the individual achieved the results and explore subtleties of performance to support our diagnostic decision. In fact 'working memory' seems to be a weakness which is almost universal across the SpLD spectrum, and its impact is far reaching.

Points to consider

- Was the task easy and fluent or was success achieved only by working very slowly, with great concentration and determination?
- Was any strategy used to support memory? Oral rehearsal, using the voice to reinforce the memory, or a visualisation strategy, seeing detail in the mind's eye? (A visualisation strategy would change the nature of the test from an auditory one into a visual one and this might have boosted the score.)
- Did other factors such as attention, concentration or anxiety have an impact?
- If scores were unexpectedly good, does the individual have training or experience in working with the type of information in the test? Was there a notable difference between different types of stimulus material – for example real words, non-words and numbers?

If the score was only achieved by sustained and substantial effort, or application of other strategies, assessors will reflect on the implications. It is unlikely the individual would be able to maintain such effort for a long period of time, therefore the score might hide potential difficulties in more sustained tasks where the demands are more complex – for example, listening and responding in class or, for the adult, taking notes in a lecture or meeting. However, caution is always required before suggesting a score is not useful or reliable.

Interesting contrasts

Is there a marked difference between results in 'short term' and 'working' memory? Individuals might be able to manage information when they simply have to recall it, but not manage the additional demands of manipulation. Look across the assessment. Is it evident that he can manage straightforward sequences but more complex ones present problems? For example, good short-term memory might support effective decoding and spelling and compensate for weaknesses elsewhere, perhaps in phonological awareness. However, weaknesses in working memory might remain apparent in more extended or more demanding literacy tasks.

Weaknesses in working memory are central to many SpLD profiles. As assessors consider working memory test results, it is important to look across the assessment for further evidence of difficulties, especially on multi-tasking activities. Do the weaknesses have an impact on day-to-day tasks, for example in reading comprehension, extended writing tasks, making notes, copying, sequencing tasks, following discussions, remembering verbal instructions?

Assessors are well advised to explore **visual memory** as an area which can provide useful additional information. Is there a marked contrast between verbal and visual memory? Remember, we mean substantial differences, not ones within normal variation. Do we see evidence of this contrast in other areas? For example, if visual memory represents the weaker domain, does the individual fail to use visual strategies for spelling? Is his reading of sight words weaker than non-words?

Phonological awareness

Good phonological awareness skills will support reading and spelling accuracy. On the other hand, weak scores in this area indicate underlying difficulties with the ability to manipulate the sounds of language, which will make reading and spelling skills much harder to gain. There is a good deal more information available than the score here, however, and many specialists will use qualitative test materials as well as standardised ones to explore this area fully. A complication is that phonological awareness can be improved through teaching and therefore basic testing might fail to expose weaknesses in those who have received extensive specialist support in the past.

Points to consider

■ Where along the path of normal phonological development did skills break down? In segmentation or blending? At the beginning, middle or end of words? Was the difficulty in isolating sounds or blending them? Or both?

■ How quickly and easily were tasks completed? Once again we are interested in both the accuracy of the skill as well as the speed and automaticity, so we can isolate the specific area of difficulty.

- Were any strategies employed to support the result? Spoken repetition or visualisation? Did knowledge of real words help him guess at some words? Any of these approaches might mean the scores need further thought.
- Did the test design influence the outcome? Did he miss a particular sound or a particular pattern which meant the test was stopped early?

Informal test results might provide some further evidence of phonological weaknesses. For example, in cases of dyslexia, an alliterative or rhyme fluency test result might be weaker than a semantic fluency test, where words must be accessed through their sound structure rather than their meaning.

Consider if the level indicated by the test standard scores are in accord with evidence elsewhere in the assessment. For example, if scores are low, we might expect to see weaknesses in 'sounding out' words for spelling and in reading, especially in unfamiliar or non-words. Sound sequencing errors might be apparent in speech. A particularly interesting contrast here is that those with specific difficulties beyond dyslexia often have strengths in this area (a useful diagnostic pointer in itself), therefore good scores are equally worthy of consideration.

Phonological processing speed

Phonological processing speed is commonly tested in rapid-naming tasks where success shows that the individual is able to retrieve and process familiar words from long-term memory satisfactorily. Fluency of word retrieval may also be apparent – for example in spoken language, using a wide range of vocabulary in writing or quickly recognising sight words.

As rapid-naming tasks make a range of demands, where scores are weak, it can be helpful to check how different elements affected the result. There are phonological but also some visual components and the timed element throws a spotlight on more subtle difficulties which are not always apparent in everyday activities. Also, contrasts might emerge between tests involving abstract information (letters and digits) and information with some meaning attached (colours and objects).

Points to consider
- Was performance consistent across all types of task or not?
- Is there evidence of slow processing of *visual* information across the assessment? Are there any visual tracking difficulties?
- Were there articulation rather than processing difficulties?

As always, an isolated view of these results is not sufficient to make conclusions. If weaknesses in rapid-naming tasks are substantial, they will be apparent elsewhere. The individual might struggle to find the words to express his thoughts when speaking or when writing, and particularly in timed conditions. Reading and writing speeds might be lower than expectations and there might be weaknesses in the ability to manage sequential information, such as alphabetical order or multiplication tables.

Visual processing speed

Good scores in tests of visual processing speed indicate the ability to process visual codes and symbols at satisfactory speeds. However, once again, the test makes demands on a range of skills and any one might have a positive or negative influence on the score. If scores are puzzling, these different aspects need to be considered.

Points to consider
- Were motor coordination or hand-eye coordination difficulties apparent? Was it the written aspect that presented the challenge? A parallel oral version of the same task might highlight this difference.
- Were visual problems evident? In tracking or orientation, for example?
- Did memory factors play a part? Was the individual able to hold onto codes or did a weak working memory mean he had constantly to re-check the information?

It will be helpful to view the results in the light of memory, phonological processing and other cognitive tests involving visual skills, again asking where strengths and weaknesses lie. Are they in the verbal or visual domain? Or both?

Information from the analysis of reading and writing will also be useful – both require easy facility with managing visual information. Weaknesses in visual processing might again be reflected in weaker reading and writing speeds, with a pattern of visually based errors in these skills.

Many individuals with SpLD face weaknesses in processing speed, whether processing verbal or visual information. Indeed for many, it is the aspect of speed that has the greatest impact on their ability to work efficiently. Where accuracy can be improved, it is often difficulties in the speed and automaticity of tasks that persist. Understanding the character of the weakness can, however, lead to more individualised recommendations.

Literacy

As literacy scores can be affected by many factors – for example, levels of ability, opportunities for learning, the quality of teaching – we must reflect on the individual context and background as we begin our interpretation of scores.

Young pupils with dyslexia are likely to have greater difficulty in learning to read than others, but an impoverished linguistic environment makes the whole process of becoming literate that much harder, even in the absence of dyslexia. There are other children with dyslexia who are able to mask early difficulties, perhaps as a result of having the opportunity to develop a wide vocabulary with much encouragement from home, strong levels of ability and lots of effort. Here difficulties might only become apparent when working at higher levels. Therefore poor levels of literacy might be part of a profile of dyslexia and wider SpLDs, but equally there could be strengths in some aspects. It should be noted that levels can vary because of a wide range of factors.

Reading

The task here is to reflect on the results of all the different types of reading tests to sort out why the reading process is not yet as accurate or fluent as expected, so that appropriate support can be provided.

Single-word reading

A good score in a single-word reading test can demonstrate the acquisition of appropriate 'sight' vocabulary – the ability to visualise whole words in memory – or well-developed decoding skills, or an effective combination of both. Careful observation, with follow-up questions, will indicate where the balance of skill lies.

In dyslexia we would expect to see characteristic weakness in word reading in most cases, or a history of difficulty with word reading, underscored by weakness in phonological abilities. Yet word reading accuracy can be improved with practice and secondary age pupils and adults might find weaknesses emerge only under time pressure, or that existing strategies break down when faced with unfamiliar language. Once again, questions are the platform for analysis.

Points to consider

- Can the individual read single-syllable words? And multi-syllable words? How easily and quickly? Compare results from timed and untimed reading. The timed conditions might highlight difficulties in working at speed, revealing slow or inaccurate reading.
- Is sound-symbol correspondence knowledge entirely secure? Does he differentiate between the vowels and pronounce vowel digraphs correctly? Does he struggle with some consonant blends – and, if so, are these at the beginning, middle or end of words? Do silent letters, 'soft' *c* or *g* confuse him? Does he recognise common letter strings such as *-our*, *-ear*, *-ight*, and common suffixes: *-ed*, *-ing*, *-ly*, *-tion*?
- How extensive is his sight vocabulary? How far does he make use of visual strategies and how successful are these?

- Can he make analogies to known words and recognise common word features, such as prefixes/suffixes?
- How does he tackle unfamiliar words? Does he sound out all the letters then blend them accurately, or does he attempt to say letter names? At what stage do decoding skills become hesitant?

Non-word reading

Comparisons between results from timed real-word and non-word reading are useful. Evenly balanced, but weak profiles might be found across the SpLD spectrum. However, some individuals have developed good sight-word skills to compensate for poor decoding – this might be revealed by a non-word reading test. It is a common pattern in dyslexia. Conversely, those whose weaknesses are centred around the visual domain might find a relative weakness in sight words while phonic decoding is good.

There will be some children and adults for whom an untimed non-word reading test can be useful. Is it the pressure of time and weaknesses in processing speed that is holding them back, or fundamental weaknesses in phonic decoding and phonological awareness?

Reading comprehension

To comprehend text, an accomplished reader will combine the skills shown in Figure 6.1.

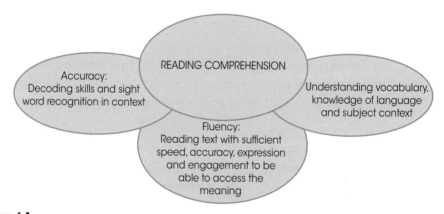

Figure 6.1

Weaknesses in one or more of these skills will interfere with efficient reading comprehension. While those with dyslexia often have problems with decoding and speed, some individuals can compensate by using sight-word strategies, context and wide language knowledge to understand what they read. Therefore, depending on the balance of strengths and weaknesses, assessors will see profiles of both weak and strong reading comprehension in those with SpLDs. The task is to identify which strategies and abilities are under-utilised and in need of strengthening. Results from reading aloud and silently will further contribute to the comprehensive picture and help identify the areas causing problems.

Points to consider

Accuracy

- From a miscue analysis (see page 173), what types of error are evident in reading aloud?
- Are weak decoding skills holding the reader back? Is he so focused on trying to read the words that he is not able to make sense of what he reads?

Fluency and Speed

- Is reading comprehension good but slow and effortful?
- Does he read fluently and smoothly with expression or not?
- Compare speed when reading aloud and silently – which is more efficient? Are the speeds appropriate for his age and stage of learning?
- Does the individual prefer to read aloud, using the sound of the voice to support memory and comprehension? Or does he always avoid reading aloud, knowing that he can absorb more of a text without having to focus on the pronunciation of words, or the performance of the reading? Compare his performance in comprehension when reading aloud and silently.

Memory

- Are working memory difficulties interfering with response to comprehension questions?
- Did the reader need to check the passage to find the answer or was he able to respond straight away?
- Did he gain the correct answer by searching for key words and then quoting verbatim, or could he express the answer in his own words?

Concentration

- Could attention and focus be maintained throughout the task?
- Was he simply not engaged or interested? If so, this could easily be the cause of a poor score.

Language

- Did the text use vocabulary and/or context that were beyond his abilities and experience, despite being age-appropriate?

Links across the assessment

- How do single-word reading skills compare with reading comprehension? Is word reading more or less accurate when the focus is also on meaning?
- Are the results from processing speed tests in accord with reading speed measures?
- Consider reading comprehension skills in the light of responses in spoken language. This will give a clue as to whether comprehension difficulties are language-based or due to a reading difficulty.
- If a listening comprehension was administered, which was stronger – listening or reading comprehension? Why? Perhaps removing the reading element enabled the individual to show his understanding fully? If both are weak, does

this suggest a language difficulty – what other evidence in the assessment might support this?

Before concluding that reading comprehension weaknesses are part of an SpLD profile, we must recall that reading for study is often difficult – many people have to re-read to understand new information. It is difficulties beyond those experienced by most students that are of interest. Weakness might also come simply from lack of reading experience and practice, or more general difficulties in learning.

Typically for those with dyslexia, reading comprehension is not an automatic process. It remains inefficient because decoding and reading for meaning persist as two separate activities and so the individual has to re-read the text, perhaps several times to manage both processes. Despite that, individuals with dyslexia might have good comprehension, particularly in contrast to their word reading skills. Individuals with other SpLDs can also face difficulties in reading comprehension due to working memory, attention, language or processing speed issues.

Spelling

Spelling is a complicated task and analysis beyond the standardised test score is essential if we are to learn about the individual profile. If errors are clearly outside those we might expect in the course of normal development, we will want to consider, once again, the particular underpinning skills which are causing problems so we can offer support. Most individuals being assessed will already know they are bad at spelling – to be useful the assessor must provide some new information!

Points to consider
- Is sound-symbol correspondence secure?
- Is the sound structure of the word accurately represented?
- Are there examples of 'bizarre' spelling?
- Are there difficulties with spelling rules?
- Are there difficulties in applying irregular or visually-based letter patterns?
- Are letters correctly formed?
- Are there fine motor coordination difficulties, resulting in illegible handwriting?
- Is spelling automatic and fluent or hesitant, slow and effortful?

The assessor will look closely for evidence of which spelling patterns and rules have been mastered and which are causing problems. For example, is there confusion between vowel sounds? Are the basic consonant digraphs (*sh, ch, th, ng*) known? Do individuals know how to tackle multi-syllable words or apply suffixing rules?

Perhaps the individual has difficulty identifying phonemes and remembering them in the correct order, so that, for example, phonemes or whole syllables are omitted, (*call* for *called*, *cole* for *could*; *musem* for *museum; beging* for *beginning*). While this demonstrates some skills, entirely dysphonetic or bizarre spelling (*sotr* for *story* at 7 years; *kelse* for *careless* at 10 years; *ianzliset* for *anxiety* at 23 years) is of greater concern.

It is helpful to report on the strategies the individual applies in spelling in order to inform teaching recommendations. Does he rely on sound-based strategies and always sound out words, or does he try visual approaches – perhaps writing the word, looking at the whole word and then trying again? Are the strategies reliable and effective or inefficient and inaccurate?

Spelling and free writing

It will be illuminating to compare single-word spelling skills with spelling in free writing.

- Does the opportunity to focus on one word at a time make spelling more accurate? Do errors emerge when the demands of composition are added? A word spelled correctly in the single-word test might well appear in multiple, different variations in free writing.
- Does he stop frequently to consider his spellings, or work slowly? Without time pressure this means his accuracy is reasonable, but the lack of fluency might interfere so substantially he struggles to put his ideas down in writing.
- Or does handwriting becomes illegible? This might be due to motor coordination difficulties, or a crafty strategy to fudge the occasions when he is unsure of the letter sequence?
- Conversely, spelling might improve in free writing. Is that because he is free to choose the words he knows he can spell? Or does contextual or grammatical knowledge help him?

Typically, spelling is a lifelong difficulty for those with dyslexia due to early and persistent phonological difficulties. They struggle to recall spelling patterns consistently, accurately and fluently. Looking more broadly across the SpLD spectrum, it might, for example, be the motor coordination or visual memory aspects of spelling which are the sources of poor spelling skills.

Free writing

The multiple demands of free writing make the interpretation of writing results challenging. Familiarity with normal development is needed alongside knowledge of the range of skills required. Writing composition requires automatic, accurate handwriting or typing, as well as organisation, memory, attention and language ability. Our task is to see if writing is confident and fluent or hesitant and inaccurate.

Points to consider

- How does his ability to write independently compare with his ability to express himself in **spoken language**?
- Is he able to express his **ideas** clearly, succinctly and effectively in writing?
- Does he use a wide or restricted **vocabulary**? Appropriate to his age or not?
- Is he able to write **accurately** in terms of spelling, punctuation and grammar?
- Is his writing logical with an effective **structure**? Are planning skills in place?
- Is he able to write fluently and at a good **speed** for his age and stage of learning, or does he write with hesitations, stopping to consider alternatives and making revisions?
- Is his handwriting **legible**? Does use of a keyboard help or hinder?

Of particular interest in any interpretation of writing skills is establishing how difficulties relate to underlying specific causes. Phonological difficulties might be expected to be reflected in spelling. Working memory problems might be evident, where individuals perhaps lose the thread of what they are writing or find their writing accuracy suffers because of multiple demands. Processing speed weaknesses might emerge in slow writing rates, or motor coordination difficulties might be reflected in poor handwriting or keyboard skills.

Copying

A copying task takes out the compositional element of writing, allowing a closer look at other component skills. If copying speed is weak, this might be due to visual processing difficulties, working memory difficulties, or poor motor coordination. Yet if copying speed is good in relation to writing, these weaknesses can perhaps be excluded and we can consider if difficulties are associated with the tasks of organising text with accuracy. Clearly, copying is still a complex task, so using information from elsewhere in the assessment will be needed to interpret the result fully. If copying speed is weak, specific recommendations will be needed for support as this skill is often needed in day-to-day life in education.

Numeracy

A standardised test score is once again only a brief start in interpreting specific difficulties relating to numeracy. Crucially we need to know whether the individual understands the mathematical concepts, *how* he solves problems and *how long* the process takes him. Discussion with the individual will be necessary.

Points to consider

- Could reading skills have been an initial barrier to success? For example, can the individual perform with greater success if word-problems are read to him?

- Did time limits of the test have a significant impact? Might he complete the problems given sufficient time?
- Did he forget his place in the problem and have to re-start several times?
- Were there left/right or layout confusions? Columns or decimal points incorrectly aligned? Was it the organisation of the material that was difficult, even though concept knowledge and method was good?
- Did he use immature counting strategies? Perhaps using fingers, or five-bar gates, to support even basic calculation?
- Did he use good verbal abilities to support him? Did he talk himself through the problem? Re-frame it in his own words?
- Is the individual exceptionally anxious? Has he avoided maths for so long that scores are bound to be weak?
- Is he simply out of practice in undertaking the type of task in the test?

Links across the assessment

- Is numeracy attainment in sharp contrast to literacy performance? Stronger or weaker? Can lack of learning opportunities or other environmental factors explain this?
- Are scores in rapid-naming tasks, working memory and processing speed tests low? Is the pattern in these scores reflected in the approaches and difficulties observed here?

In cases of dyslexia, we might see that individuals have a good grasp of number concepts but struggle with mental arithmetic, working quickly, reading questions and interpreting the language of maths, retrieving and working with sequences. More pervasive maths problems and possibly a specific difficulty in this domain will arise when conceptual understanding is weak and fundamental skills and strategies fail to be applied. Reflection on definitions and the relative balance within the individual profile will be needed to allow assessors to decide on appropriate diagnostic labels.

English as an Additional Language (EAL)

EAL issues add complexities to the assessment interpretation. Therefore, if we have agreed to proceed with the assessment (see Chapter 5), we must consider a broader range of factors, especially those demanding language skills, before coming to a diagnostic conclusion.

Points to consider

- Are there weaknesses in the first language that suggest a developmental difficulty exists? Consider both reported early learning difficulties and also the findings from tests measuring speed of working in the first language – cognitive processing and reading and writing speeds. For an SpLD to be present, we would expect weaknesses here.

- Did the individual apply a strategy of translating between languages to undertake tasks? If yes, this calls on very substantial processing resources and might explain weak test results.
- Have differences in the first language been excluded as reasons for weaknesses in tests conducted in English?
- The phonology of the first language may be quite different from English. There may be a significantly different number and range of phonemes. If the language does not contain a particular sound, individuals might have difficulty in hearing the differences in English and this could affect results in phonological and literacy tests.
- If individuals consistently mispronounce or confuse particular sounds in their speech, this will affect how they deal with those sounds in reading and spelling; vowel pronunciation can be particularly vulnerable when English is not the first language. Were there any evident patterns in spoken language that might explain test results?
- The first language might be one with a simple syllable structure and a transparent phoncme-grapheme orthography, as in Spanish, or have a more complex syllable construction, as in German. Has the approach of the first language been applied to English? Or the first language might have no alphabetic or logographic orthography, using a pictorial script instead, as in Chinese.
- The grammar may be quite different. Perhaps grammatical errors might be the result of following this alternative structure rather than any specific difficulty in processing language?
- How long has the individual been living in the UK or studying in English? Has he had sufficient opportunity to develop wider language abilities? Weaker underlying verbal ability measures must be used cautiously. Also, spoken fluency comes before written fluency, so relative weakness in the latter might be due to a normal process of learning. If a long history of English learning is in place, yet difficulties and contrasts persist, we have greater grounds to consider an SpLD.
- What pattern emerges from the tests where there is less cultural bias and fewer language demands? Visual processing speed, non-verbal ability and short-term and working memory tests using a digit span task are less culture-related. Weaknesses in the cognitive processing measures might be expected.

Synchronising the evidence

Before we apply a diagnostic label, we need to be confident that there exists a substantial weight of evidence to support the naming of a specific learning difficulty, having set aside all the possible interferences.

At the end of this process where we have considered all the detail, we must pull the information together. Having eliminated all other possible causes for the difficulties, can we conclude that an SpLD is present, and apply a diagnostic label? If we can, we should be able to see how all of the data fits together in a consistent and coherent way to support our conclusion. If some aspect appears to be out of place, this is the area which needs further thought, testing or questioning until the reason becomes apparent. Whatever the diagnostic conclusion, we will have a wealth of detailed information about the individual's strengths and weaknesses on which to base our recommendations.

Perspectives on assessment profiles

We have already considered a good number of links across the assessment tasks. We can now take a broader perspective and consider some basic patterns, although these will still be viewed through the lens of background and context.

- If results from the cognitive assessment, including underlying ability, working memory, processing speed and phonological skills, are reasonably balanced, and attainment measures are broadly in line with these, there would be insufficient evidence for a specific learning difficulty.

- If the scores in the cognitive measures are reasonably consistent, but scores in attainment measures are low, then it would seem that there was some other interference with the acquisition of these skills rather than an SpLD. Further investigation would be needed. Conversely, if attainment measures are higher, it would seem not to be a case of dyslexia, but rather that the individual has worked hard to build their literacy skills.

- However, if the cognitive measures present an unusual and inconsistent profile of weaknesses, especially in the areas of working memory, processing speed and phonological abilities, and it can be seen that these deficits are the cause of difficulties observed and they have a marked impact on attainment, this would indicate a pattern consistent with a specific learning difficulty.

Assessors must then decide upon an appropriate diagnostic label which best describes the profile and supports the individual. To help in this decision, the next chapter presents some descriptive assessment outlines which aim to support assessors as they reflect on their data in each case.

Summary

- Effective assessment is about drawing together information from a wide range of sources. The observations and qualitative interpretations of the assessor are vital.

- A process of reflection on each test score and how it was achieved is necessary for accurate interpretation. Themes will emerge and these are used to make diagnostic decisions.

- In all cases, whether or not an SpLD is identified, the pattern of strengths and weaknesses which emerges from careful interpretation will guide recommendations for supporting the individual.

With each assessment carried out, the assessor will build up experience and skills and gain in confidence. But have patience! It is a complex process. Being able to discuss a tricky profile with a colleague is immensely valuable. Therefore we recommend all assessors, at whatever stage of their career, build up contacts and have the support of colleagues or mentors so profiles can be shared, discussed and used to inform continuing professional development.

7 Assessment Profiles – Making Diagnostic Decisions

In our work as assessors, we will meet a never-ending variety of scores – there will be no one person with exactly the same background, educational experience, teaching input, set of abilities, achievements and set of results as another. Thus, it is clear individuals will not fit exactly into neat diagnostic boxes. However, in spite of all the variation, if there is a specific learning difficulty present, we will meet recognisable patterns which respond to theoretical frameworks.

The high levels of co-occurrence and overlap between SpLDs can make diagnostic decisions complex. The best approach will be to identify the dominant core features, and use these to decide on the appropriate diagnostic label. Where additional, but peripheral, SpLD-type difficulties exist, these features can be described without further diagnostic names. However, if other core conditions co-exist, it might be appropriate to identify an additional diagnostic label, but with a note to the effect that co-occurrence is common. We must always consider if any additional label is fully justified and supports the individual and, in all cases, go on to describe the presenting difficulties and make appropriate recommendations.

If, on close reflection, in cases of complex profiles there is no dominant pattern, a diagnostic conclusion of 'Specific Learning Difficulties' is likely to be useful, and this is often acceptable to education and funding authorities. It does mean that assessors must still explain clearly the underlying difficulties and their impact on performance. However, this conclusion could be more useful than an extended list of different diagnostic labels.

To help clarify the diagnostic boundaries, the following broad descriptions of some typical patterns of assessment scores and features are offered for comparative purposes. We have deliberately kept these brief and focussed on 'classic' profiles so that they demonstrate the outline shape of a particular SpLD, but they are not intended as diagnostic checklists. Assessors can use them as a starting point against which to compare their own results and review which elements are dominant. Assessors will decide if a particular diagnostic label is appropriate, based on their knowledge of theory and the individual. *Throughout, we describe characteristic weaknesses but recognise that individuals might also have a host of strengths and these should be noted when opportunity arises.*

Once again, do remember, everyone in the general population has a range of abilities, with contrasting strengths and weaknesses. Before concluding an SpLD is present, we need to be certain that the differences we find are those that fall outside normal variation.

Dyslexia

In cases of dyslexia we expect to find a history of difficulty in literacy skills. There are most likely to have been difficulties with the acquisition of reading and spelling skills in the early years of school. Reports might refer to problems in reading books as expected, in handwriting, in writing accurately and at sufficient length, in spending hours on homework, or not being able to finish work in time. Often, as educational demands increase, the difficulties manifest more clearly. The volume of reading and writing tasks is likely to cause difficulty and working under pressure and timed conditions is a continuing challenge.

Perhaps the most telling diagnostic feature of dyslexia is an underlying weakness in phonological awareness. Assessors are likely to find that tests of rhyme and alliteration, or segmenting, blending and manipulating sounds, show weakness. In addition, we expect to find weaknesses in phonological and visual processing speed as well as working memory. Scores in the verbal domain could be weaker than in the visual one. The combination of difficulties can in some cases mean that in the longer term, underlying verbal abilities develop less effectively than expected and present a contrast with non-verbal skills.

These cognitive weaknesses will likely lead to a range of difficulties. They might include inaccuracies in reading, particular difficulties in non-word reading, slow reading speed, and effortful reading comprehension – although in relation to word reading accuracy, reading comprehension might be stronger. Difficulties with written language are likely to be present or become more apparent as demands increase. Spelling accuracy is often an ongoing problem, especially in free writing. Weaknesses in writing might also emerge – for example, in grammar, organisation and structure, speed of output, perhaps in contrast to good creative ideas and content.

Written language skills are often noticeably poorer than spoken language skills, but sometimes language processing difficulties remain evident in speech. There might be evidence of hesitations, revisions of expression or word-finding difficulties, especially if the individual is under pressure or put 'on the spot'.

The balance of skills, strengths and weaknesses will change over time. For example, while reading might become more accurate, reading speed and written composition might remain problematic.

Individuals with dyslexia might also describe some difficulties in organisation, as well as perhaps elements of difficulty in motor coordination. These are common features of dyslexia but, if difficulties here appear substantial, assessors might consider the possibility of other specific difficulties and investigate further.

Dyspraxia

In cases of dyspraxia there will be a confirmed history of significant motor coordination difficulty. There is likely to have been difficulty with early motor tasks – for example, crawling, feeding and dressing. Difficulties will also emerge at school. Individual sports are more likely to be pursued than team games involving throwing, catching or nifty footwork, and children and adults with dyspraxia are prone to bump into things, drop things and trip up more frequently than expected. These gross motor difficulties most often go alongside fine motor problems, for example in handwriting and activities such as cutting and keyboard skills. However, the picture changes over time. Perhaps individuals learn to be especially careful with their movement, or determinedly and repeatedly practise their favourite sport or hobby over and over again, without realising others do not have to give the same degree of effort.

Difficulties in planning and organisation are key features of dyspraxia. Managing school timetables, or planning the time needed for work is difficult. Keeping paperwork in order is a constant challenge and the organisation of daily life is a task to be actively managed; there are many reports of lost possessions – sports kit, phones and keys. While descriptions will vary, problems with organisation across a range of activities will consistently emerge.

Further evidence of the difficulties of dyspraxia will be found in the cognitive profile. It is likely that deficits in visual processing speed will emerge, often particularly noticeable in tasks involving writing. Phonological processing speed is also likely to be weak, although phonological awareness and short-term verbal memory are likely to be good. Working memory will probably present as a significant area of weakness; this might be more pronounced in the visual domain but is equally possible in verbal tasks. Similarly, underlying language abilities might be relatively stronger than visual reasoning or visual-spatial abilities, although this is not universally the case. Overall, in the cognitive and attainment profile a pattern of relative strength in the verbal domain might emerge in comparison to a pattern of relative weakness in visual skills and abilities.

The combination of difficulties will present quite a different attainment profile from one of dyslexia. Single-word reading accuracy might be good, supported by secure phonological awareness – assessors might find relative strengths in non-word reading compared to sight-word reading at speed, but reading comprehension might be weaker, because of the organisational demands needed to link language and meaning. Writing tasks might be challenging because of the structural elements, grammar and punctuation, and the organisation of words in sentences and ideas in the whole. Where spelling difficulties do exist – and this is common – it is due to the visual and motor elements of the task rather than the phonological ones. It is likely that processing speed weaknesses also lead to slow reading and writing speeds, and difficulty in absorbing new information quickly.

There may well be difficulty with the visual-spatial and sequencing demands of number work and mathematics.

Dyscalculia

A profile of dyscalculia will include a weak score in a standardised arithmetic computation test, but it is essential for assessors to seek much more information. A long and probably painful history of difficulty with learning number, going back to early primary school, will be evident alongside continuing difficulty with everyday numeracy – for example, children have inordinate difficulty in grasping one-to-one correspondence, in learning to tell the time, and difficulties here might persist. Equally, handling money is difficult and calculating change likely to be extremely challenging.

Poorly developed, immature and unreliable strategies in tackling numeracy tasks will be observed, with very slow speeds of working, alongside difficulty in quickly retrieving number facts – for example, the child with dyscalculia will have found times tables impossible, number bonds a mystery, and have continued to use finger-counting strategies when his peers would not. Even when his calculation is correct, he may be very unsure of his answer. Crucially, although he might learn to apply methods by rote, he is unlikely to be able to explain the reasoning behind them, or apply them flexibly and so will not spot when these go wrong, particularly as estimation skills tend to be very weak.

Weaknesses in working memory will probably emerge – and results of visual memory tests might be weaker than those of verbal memory. Processing speeds, especially in digit-based tasks, might be low, but not necessarily. Test results are likely to reveal weaker non-verbal than verbal abilities. Tasks of all kinds involving number are likely to reveal relative weaknesses in comparison to those involving language. All these remain matters for research, therefore great caution and care is needed, and readers will see that the detail of the case history and observation of how individuals tackle tasks are very much at the core of diagnostic decisions here.

Where dyscalculia seems to be the dominant difficulty, phonological awareness and literacy skills are likely to be commensurate with expectations, fine and gross motor skills good, attention and concentration appropriate. However, co-occurrence rates with other SpLDs are considerable and therefore the potential for overlapping characteristics is high.

Specific language impairment (SLI)

Early speech and language development is likely to have been sufficiently delayed to have been noted by parents and teachers. The case history will probably also reveal that the child has problems using language effectively – perhaps he does not respond as expected to the language of the classroom and the playground

– frequently misunderstanding or being misunderstood by adults and peers. This might lead not only to difficulties in learning, but social, emotional and behavioural difficulties. As the child or young person struggles to communicate effectively with those around them, some might become withdrawn or isolated.

Tests of receptive and expressive language will present an unusual profile and both areas might be very weak, or one domain might show a notable deficiency. Overall, verbal abilities can be expected to be lower than non-verbal abilities. Phonological difficulties will probably emerge alongside problems with short-term and working memory and word-finding difficulties are common.

Difficulties with the meaning and structure of language will be evident in both spoken and written language and assessors will observe inaccurate use of grammar. A careful analysis of written construction will be necessary, and tests measuring understanding of grammatical construction might prove useful in some cases. Language problems will make reading comprehension especially weak, as individuals are less able to draw on context to support understanding, and in most cases this will also mean listening comprehension is impaired. Assessment results will show weaknesses in single-word reading, of both sight words and non-words, and reading and writing speeds will be slow, although the profile of spelling skills is likely to be unpredictable and complex. However, most literacy problems are rooted in phonological rather than visual difficulties. Referral to a speech and language therapist will be needed to come to a diagnostic conclusion.

Assessors will observe many similar characteristics to those of dyslexia, as there is a great deal of overlap here. The key differences lie in the use of language in spoken and written form: an individual with dyslexia has generally grasped the correct grammatical structure of language, often has strong verbal abilities and spoken language skills, and may be a relatively effective communicator.

There are high co-occurrence rates with other SpLDs such as dyspraxia and ADHD, but language impairment is also associated with general learning difficulties and autism spectrum disorders. Therefore, profiles are likely to be complex.

Attention deficit hyperactivity disorder

In cases where we observe substantial problems with attention, as educational specialists, we can describe the difficulties in learning and the impact on performance and make recommendations, but – especially in the case of children – referrals for further assessment must be made to specialist medical practitioners, often sourced through the GP, as symptoms of ADHD may also be caused by the presence of undiagnosed medical conditions. Such referrals open up the way for medical treatment as well as other support and management.

If there are significant concerns with attention, it is essential that the assessor has suitable training or experience in this area and is alert to typical characteristics. ADHD can affect school and work performance, self-esteem, and the quality and duration of relationships – friendships can be hard to build and maintain from an early age. Therefore assessors will attempt to take into account the difficulties which interfere with multiple aspects of life, not just school or study activities. These difficulties will also be evident in the past history of the individual, going well beyond those common issues with concentration and attention across all SpLDs. The profile is likely to feature characteristics such as:

- impulsivity: inability to inhibit thought, response or action;
- daydreaming; falling into reveries; failing to pay attention;
- sustaining attention on any one task;
- being easily distracted by internal or external stimuli;
- feeling constantly restless and compelled to get up and move around;
- difficulty settling to and then sustaining attention on reading and writing tasks;
- having problems completing tasks and meeting deadlines;
- difficulties with procrastination and decision making;
- significant problems with organisation and time-keeping;
- inability to be motivated and engage in an activity in spite of intention;
- inability to vary attention according to need – if an activity does engage interest, focus might be intense and the individual oblivious to time passing.
- problems with sleeping patterns;
- having feelings of isolation, and ongoing problems with self-confidence, anxiety and low mood.

The cognitive profile is not easy to typify. There are often difficulties in speed of processing, and problems with working memory, but they might only emerge in more extended or complex tasks. However, while speed in academically related tasks is often slow, sometimes, perhaps in more creative respects, it might be very fast indeed. When ADHD occurs on its own, we would not expect to see weaknesses in phonological awareness, motor coordination or language acquisition. However, once again co-occurring difficulties with other SpLDs are very common, and frequent overlaps with mental health difficulties occur, including, for example, anxiety and mood disorders, especially depression.

Complicating factors: low underlying ability and dyslexia

We know that dyslexia can affect people across the ability ranges and there is no clear cut-off point between specific and more general learning difficulties. Yet the lower the ability levels, the more the dyslexia difficulties become inextricably interwoven with more general difficulties, until it becomes impossible to tease them apart and the identification of a dyslexia profile becomes unreliable. What is paramount is that we must sift all the evidence very carefully and be certain that a specific learning difficulty is present before giving such a diagnostic label.

When there is a fairly even profile of scores across the set of test results, it suggests that the difficulties experienced are not 'specific' ones. In some profiles with low underlying ability, there might be significant deficits in working memory, processing speed and phonology. However, where individuals have problems with wider learning, it becomes increasingly difficult to say with confidence that difficulties in skill acquisition are a result of these underlying deficits of dyslexia – and we know that, statistically, test results present greater problems at their extremes. The background might show a broad history of struggle in literacy, memory and learning, difficulties in keeping up with demands of the curriculum, and in learning new tasks.

Sometimes the pattern of attainment scores in those with low ability is the reverse of the pattern of a dyslexia profile. Reading and spelling levels at the single-word level can be higher than other scores, and skills have become competent through determined and persistent effort. Yet reading comprehension, and writing skills, where the cognitive demands are greater, remain weak. A visual processing speed score can be reasonably good because, again, the task makes demands on a one-to-one relationship in a code and this is manageable, while a more complex visual reasoning task is not. Similarly verbal short-term memory might be good, but working memory weaker.

Dyslexia may make it more difficult to acquire vocabulary knowledge and verbal reasoning skills, but those with more general difficulties will also have difficulty with acquiring vocabulary knowledge and being able to reason using language. If the only relative strength of underlying ability is in a practical task of non-verbal ability, and not a reasoning task, be cautious. Just as we would not want to identify dyslexia on one single deficit, or one low score, nor would we want to identify dyslexia because there was one single score which was relatively stronger.

Complicating factors: high ability and dyslexia

In those with high ability, we expect to see similar sharp contrasts in the cognitive scores, in the pattern of strengths and weakness, alongside qualitative evidence from the observations and history as those with average abilities. If the contrasts and evidence are substantial, then a specific learning difficulty can be present. Difficulties might not have been identified in the past if individuals were able to successfully compensate using other strengths. Indeed, it might be the increasing demands of their studies as they move through school or university that expose underlying weaknesses. In these cases, reading and spelling accuracy skills might have developed to reasonable levels in standardised tests; however, assessors might observe persisting unexpected errors in text-level skills – small miscues in reading, spelling errors in common words. Able individuals are often able to apply strategies and different approaches to learning, but difficulties persist in the fluency, speed and automaticity of skills and the management and organisation of large amounts of written information. Reading comprehension can demand continued effort and writing composition many re-drafts and re-workings.

8 Recommendations and Working with Others

Without useful recommendations, a diagnostic report is close to worthless. A controversial statement, perhaps, but even the most careful diagnostic analysis must be followed by well-founded suggestions, which match individual needs and reflect the findings of the assessment. This is much more valuable than the confirmation of a diagnostic label.

The ultimate aim of all recommendations is to promote independence. What new skills or strategies would be useful and what support should be provided so that this young person or adult can move forward? To answer these questions effectively, we will use knowledge of underpinning development processes as well as all the information about the individual gathered in the assessment – his strengths, weaknesses, goals, context, and so on. To identify all the areas to be considered, assessors might work through the following set of questions.

What strengths have been found?	Can these talents be used to support other skills? Or should they be noted in the recommendations to ensure they are encouraged? A talented young designer does not wish his favourite art lesson to be removed from his timetable for extra spelling.
What does the individual already know?	What stage in skill development has he reached?
What weaknesses have been found?	Where do skills break down? Where does he lack confidence and fluency? Where are the gaps in his understanding, knowledge or skill? In what order do these skills need to be learned?
What is achievable?	What timeframe are the recommendations to cover? What time and energy does he have to give to learning? How will this fit into his current situation?
How might the learning history affect the next step?	It is vital to consider past learning history so methods that have already failed are not repeated. New approaches, styles or contexts must be found to address persisting difficulties.
What are the current concerns? What needs to be learned?	Do the recommendations address the difficulties currently being faced, but also balance them against needs for underpinning knowledge? Young people and adults will respond well to an explanation of why they should begin at a certain point as long as their end goal is always borne in mind.
What are the aims, dreams, aspirations, interests of the individual?	This is more than just his 'needs'. Too many recommendations fail to consider their recipients – even very young children can contribute ideas about what they enjoy to give a context for teaching and much motivation.

In which contexts and situations does the individual need support? Where is he facing problems?	At school, this might most commonly be the classroom but could take many other forms: science labs, playing fields, music rooms, for example. Vocational and employment contexts present even more variety.
What might he need in the future?	What new challenges might appear in his next school? Or college? Or job? These questions will be addressed to different degrees, depending on the imminence of the transition.
Who will be involved in delivering these recommendations?	What do all the different people involved in supporting this individual need to know and understand to be effective?
What is reasonable and achievable?	What systems and resources are available (or should be made available) to help him? What is possible? Recommendations must be practical and within the limits of real-world provision, while still seeking excellence in support.

To ensure recommendations flow directly from the evidence and retain an individual character, a structured approach to reflection on strengths and weaknesses might be of value.

- List each skill and ability investigated (reading, writing, spelling, working memory, phonological processing, verbal ability, spoken language skill, etc, as appropriate to the case).
- Against each skill, first note the strengths and their implications for teaching. Active consideration here will ensure the report does not become a catalogue of weaknesses. Think of existing levels of knowledge, skills, interests and strategies already in use.
- Next, note the weaknesses in each skill/ability area. This will provide clear direction to what needs to be developed and supported.

There is, of course, no simple, direct relationship between one test outcome and one recommendation, as skills are so closely entwined. One test result may have implications across a wide range of activities – consider the wide impact of a weak working memory, or phonological awareness, for example.

The most important thing is that **recommendations respond to the key features of the profile that have been used to identify the SpLD**. We give a few examples below for a flavour of the process, but specialist assessors with experience of teaching will be particularly well placed to reflect on the links between assessment data and strategies.

- Weaknesses in **phonological awareness** and **verbal short-term memory**, particularly in the case of younger people, would suggest a need for work at an appropriate level, such as on onset-rime; phonological syllabification, letter patterns to support decoding, use of sound-symbol correspondence in spelling. We will have noted difficulties in those skills but could also anticipate problems in vocabulary learning, perhaps particularly in a foreign language. Therefore recommendations for a structured, multisensory learning approach will be valuable in this area.

- Weaknesses in **processing speed**, which impact on reading and writing speed and/or fluency, might suggest recommendations to work on text-level reading strategies, and use of supported reading and writing, both human and computer-based.
- Weaknesses in **working memory** would suggest recommendations for chunking and recording strategies of all kinds – including those for teachers to use. Advice on inclusive practice here – for example, using direct language, giving instructions in short bursts, providing written back up, etc – would be beneficial, as well as techniques for the individual, depending on his difficulties – perhaps reading comprehension, writing composition, note-taking or mathematics.
- Weaknesses in **verbal ability** might suggest the need for vocabulary development through supported reading/listening, the use of audio books and support with specific subject vocabulary for writing topics. **Strengths in verbal ability**, but weakness in decoding, would suggest a recommendation for opportunities to continue to enjoy literature at an appropriately high level without the pressure of reading to support continued learning – listening comprehension or computer-supported reading.
- Stronger **receptive than expressive vocabulary** will likely characterise the individual who finds difficulties expressing himself on paper. Recommendations for planning writing might include identifying key words before beginning, and creating personal subject specific dictionaries.

Having decided on the recommendations, they should be set out in clearly headed sections in the report so that those who need them can find them easily. The following categories are likely to be useful for those in education – they can always be adjusted to fit individual circumstances.

- Specialist teaching and support
- Classroom / mainstream / general academic support and adjustments
- Assistive technology
- Examination access arrangements
- Strategies at home
- Future considerations – especially when transition to a new context is foreseeable
- Further referrals – much more occasionally.

Specialist teaching and support recommendations

In many cases, one-to-one specialist SpLD support is recommended and, especially for children and young people, a detailed teaching plan prepared (see page 178 for the key features of a teaching programme). For older students, or indeed those beyond education, there might not be a need for a formal teaching programme, but all will be interested in understanding strategies or ideas for different ways of working to help them become more efficient.

Regardless of the age or stage of the individual, the key principle to apply is that all teaching recommendations should embrace multisensory techniques. Even older learners are often very willing to use multisensory approaches, provided that their purpose and rationale is explained.

Classroom/mainstream/general academic support and adjustments

While programmes for individuals are important, so too are clear and reasonable recommendations for inclusive practice. Good practice in the mainstream classroom can make all the difference between miserable school days or enjoyable and successful ones.

Be ready to suggest ideas for different ways of giving instructions, presenting, recording and storing information, completing tasks, adapting tasks and goals, and so on, to support individual weaknesses. For just one example: copying down homework quickly at the end of a lesson is a perennial difficulty, but an electronic or printed-out homework record enables pupils, and their parents, to have an accurate record of what is to be done and can eliminate much frustration on all sides.

Classroom support might also extend to small-group activities or work with a teaching assistant and the assessor can suggest areas or skills where such work would be valuable. The assessor will have outlined the skill areas which need developing in specialist sessions and this work can be reviewed and reinforced in the classroom.

Assistive technology

IT-based tools and materials might feature in specialist teaching and classroom recommendations – their value cannot be ignored. These might include SpLD specific resources or the technology available for pockets, school bags and briefcases (mobile phones, etc). Assessors might find their younger clients are far more familiar with the latest applications but, as difficult as it might appear to be, it is important to keep up to date with available technologies – or know someone who is!

Examination access arrangements

A key purpose of many assessments is to investigate the need for access arrangements in examinations, so recommendations here are common. When making decisions, it is necessary not just to consider test scores, but also the individual history of performance in examinations, current ways of working, and the individual's preferences. Individuals should be made aware that assessors are not the final arbiters of arrangements and that the prevailing examination body regulations will determine the outcome. Even if the key purpose of assessment is examination considerations, assessors should also take this opportunity to make recommendations for development wherever possible – an access arrangement should not be all that a learner sees by way of support. At minimum, guidance and practice will be needed in how best to use the arrangements.

Recommendations for outside school

Where appropriate, consideration should be given to making recommendations for individuals to work on at home.

Parents would likely welcome suggestions of games or activities to support their child, as well as the more traditional (and often less exciting) reading and spelling practice. Parents can also be advised of supportive organisational strategies and routines to avoid panic and confusion – such as keeping timetables to show on which days sports kit is needed, or setting a time limit to homework, in agreement with the school. Also, parents can often offer non-academic support, such as opportunities for sports, artistic or creative activities, which build up self-esteem and might provide an area in which to demonstrate a skill.

Older students could be directed to self-help strategies or resources. This might include, for example, alternative approaches to reading and writing, ways to become organised or reduce stress, innovative approaches to revision, or guidance to good websites with new ideas for successful learning and so on.

Future directions

Assessors can also consider the likely impact of an individual's specific difficulties on the next stage in their journey – whether it is school, college or work. Transitions are known to be especially challenging for those with SpLDs – different tasks, new places, more demands, and less support all might feature. Signposts to key steps to take, resources to refer to, or people to contact will be very useful.

Working with other professionals

Making further assessment referrals

A key part of professional practice is recognising when to call on the support of other professionals. Close teamwork between professionals can throw a new light on the problems being faced – although the dreadful prospect of an individual going from one professional to the next, without coordination, and possibly gathering a new label at every visit, must be avoided at all costs. There is therefore a balance to be achieved between exhaustive investigation and assessment fatigue. At some point, earlier rather than later, we must simply get on with helping the person before us.

With children and young adults, it is important to liaise closely with the SENCO and parents when making these decisions. In some cases, recommendations for a range of in-school support strategies might be employed, without the need for subjecting the individual to more assessment. However, Table 8.1 provides a useful starting point to consider where referral might be useful – in some cases it will be absolutely necessary.

Other professionals	Referral for:
Educational Psychologists	complex cases of multiple difficulties extending beyond SpLD emotional/behavioural issues child and family guidance issues
Speech and Language Therapist	unclear speech; problems with articulation language development – delay or disorder? social communication difficulties
Paediatrician/GP (these professionals might then refer to other specialists and services)	possible developmental delay possible medical conditions possible autistic spectrum disorder any recent sudden deterioration in motor skills mental health concerns possible attention deficit disorder (ADHD)
Paediatric Physiotherapist or Occupational Therapist	concerns regarding motor coordination difficulties
Behavioural Optometrist	concerns regarding visual acuity/comfort/perception, squint, etc. potential severe visual stress
Audiologist	hearing difficulties/auditory processing

Table 8.1

Educational psychologists

Work with an educational psychologist might become necessary if there are complexities in the case such that the assessor would value a second opinion. Perhaps difficulties extend outside the assessor's experience or beyond the SpLD domain. Educational psychologists have access to a range of tests and assessment materials that are 'closed' to teachers which might provide further dimension to an analysis.

Speech and language therapists

Speech and language therapists, with their detailed understanding of processes of speech and language development, can offer invaluable advice. Assessments are likely to include vocabulary, comprehension, grammatical rules, conversational skills, descriptive and explanatory ability, phonological and auditory processing skills. If a learner has been in school for some time, the assessment may also include reading and spelling. Analysis of results can have implications for planning a learning programme. In addition to providing advice and exercises for a learner's articulation, phonological skills and basic language, speech and language therapists have expertise in identifying subtler, higher-level language problems and can give advice on strategies to ameliorate them.

Occupational therapists/physiotherapists

Many individuals with SpLDs are observed to have difficulties in fine and gross motor skills; some of these might subsequently be found to have dyspraxia. Early indicators of difficulties might include poor muscle tone, clumsy/inflexible movement, avoidance of mid-line crossing, left–right confusion and bilateral integration problems (difficulty in coordinating both body sides). Where such problems are observed, young learners might be referred to an occupational therapist (OT) for assessment. The OT can offer recommendations for direct therapy, or school- and home-based programmes. Some schools have found it beneficial to organise small-group sessions, supervised by an appropriately trained support assistant, to implement the OT recommendations. Where dyspraxia seems to be the prevailing difficulty, whilst it is important that motor coordination issues are addressed, the educational impact must also be noted and supported.

For adults, availability of these services is more restricted. However, it might be the case that this type of work is no longer necessary. If study and literacy skills are the current concerns, the specialist teacher can make appropriate recommendations to address those needs.

In all cases, assessors must be alert to the potential reasons beyond SpLD that might underlie motor difficulties. If in doubt, GP referral is strongly advised so medical conditions can be excluded, and is essential in cases where recent deterioration in motor skills is noted.

Collaboration and feedback

Assessment, as we noted at the outset, is best when viewed as a partnership with the individual and those working most closely with him. Collaboration is needed in gathering background information when planning the assessment and it is immensely valuable for this work to continue afterwards. It might also be the case that further discussion or more detailed interpretation of the diagnostic report is needed, before the best way forward can be decided upon. Later, reviews of progress and emerging needs might consider which recommendations and strategies worked best and what was not helpful. Therefore, it is worth reflecting on the role of effective teamwork in assessment. For good practice there is a need to:

- develop links with key personnel in schools and colleges;
- understand and respect the roles of others involved;
- employ patience, tact and diplomacy; and
- ensure ongoing and efficient interaction between all involved.

The value of inclusive teaching is widely recognised and class teachers and college lecturers are required to understand and respond to the needs of all members of their classes. Specialist assessors are therefore often likely to be guiding others. Personal contact will help to build understanding over time as well as give information about specific cases.

Therefore effective relationships with those professionals responsible for delivering support – particularly the SENCO, inclusion manager, or additional learning support manager – will be important. While professionals like their knowledge and experience to be recognised, requests for information and offers of advice should be measured with care and conducted with respect. Professional courtesy, patience, tact and diplomacy are always appreciated.

Parents too are vital partners to ensure a childhood assessment is valuable. It is well established that where parents are involved in their child's education, outcomes are more positive. Parents can make valuable contributions to reviews of progress, and where parents, schools and assessors work together closely, it is more likely that the child's needs will be identified as they occur, be effectively addressed and therefore alleviate anxiety and stress for all.

Overall, the whole is more than the sum of the parts. An individual with a specific difficulty is fortunate indeed if he is in an environment where professionals work together and he can receive both individual and inclusive support.

Face-to-face feedback

The value of discussing the assessment findings and recommendations cannot be underestimated. In the next chapter, we discuss the diagnostic assessment report in some detail, but the opportunity to explain, in person, the findings and their implications should be taken whenever possible. Understanding of difficulties is a powerful factor in success and this step brings the detailed assessment to a proper close.

Summary

- Recommendations should respond to the key features of the profile which identified the SpLD and should be closely tailored to the individual's needs, both for the present and for any forthcoming transition.
- Multisensory teaching principles should underpin recommendations.
- Individual strategies and classroom/environmental adjustments should be considered.
- Collaboration with other professionals supporting the individual is vital, and further referral for assessment is sometimes necessary.
- Feedback and interpretation will include the written report, but also informal discussion with the individual and the provision of advice and guidance to those teaching or supporting him.

9 Writing the Assessment Report

After conducting the assessment and analysing the evidence, the next step is to write the report – a crucial part of the feedback process. The words chosen to describe the assessment findings have immense power to enhance or damage someone's self-esteem and self-confidence, consequently they must be chosen with all due care.

Therefore, in this chapter we are chiefly concerned with considering the language that is appropriate for a report. Following some general principles, we will describe a suggested format and then reflect on each section of the report. One overriding theme will soon emerge: accessibility.

General principles of report writing

The effective report has three key qualities: it is accurate, it meets the needs of its audience and it is accessible.

The report has little integrity if it is not accurate and consistent: by this we mean test scores are calculated and reported correctly and the qualitative data is honest, authoritative, and drawn from reliable and verifiable sources, rather than based on conjecture. For example, is a difficulty solely reported by a pupil or does his teacher agree? Have copies of any previously conducted assessments been seen or is this reported information?

Remember, accuracy extends to spelling, grammar and punctuation – developing a personal proof-reading strategy is essential.

With the exception of the young child, the report is written first and foremost for the individual who has been assessed. Yet the wider audience might extend to parents, class teachers, teaching assistants, other specialist teachers, other professionals, examinations officers, employers, local education authority staff, government funding bodies and – although we might hope it never to be the case – lawyers in a tribunal or court. This diversity calls for clear writing which provides the information each group needs in an accessible format.

As most report readers will have little previous knowledge of SpLDs, a text which can be understood by the non-specialist is the goal. Where specialist language is necessary, terms can be explained as they are introduced, with jargon and acronyms avoided. Even a term in common use in school might be unfamiliar to a parent. An accessible style does not, however, allow for an informal or chatty tone. At all times use a professional approach and write in the third person: *'The following tests were administered'* sounds much more professional than *'I asked Jack if he would do the reading test next.'* Finally, do adopt a positive style, without being patronising, even when difficult issues are to be addressed. The guiding principle is honesty – but not the brutal variety. It is clear that report writing is a demanding task. The best way forward is to have a structured plan in place and we present one below. As with any good plan, it can always be changed as necessary.

The report structure and format

We recommend that all assessors adopt the national guidance in regard to the structure of the report (see www.sasc.org.uk). It represents a useful framework, but still leaves room to make additions to reflect individual needs.

When writing, do also consider the overall length of the report. The document must be sufficiently detailed but also concise – most readers, especially those with reading difficulties, are unlikely to welcome endless pages of dense prose. Ensure the presentation is professional and avoid small fonts, cramped paragraphs, full justification and overuse of bold, italics and capitalisation.

Cover sheet

Introduce the 'Diagnostic Assessment Report' with a confidence-inspiring heading of 'Confidential' prominently displayed alongside details of the individual and also of the assessor, so follow-up enquiries can be made easily.

> ## Main Sections of a Diagnostic Assessment Report
>
> Cover sheet
>
> Summary
>
> Background Information
>
> Test Conditions
>
> Attainments
> - Reading Accuracy, Comprehension, Fluency and Speed
> - Reading Summary
> - Spelling
> - Writing
> - Writing Summary
>
> Cognitive Abilities
> - Underlying Cognitive Abilities
> - Cognitive Processing Abilities
>
> Other Information
>
> Conclusions
>
> Recommendations
>
> Assessor Signature
>
> Appendix 1: Summary of test results
>
> Appendix 2: Test references

A contents list might be added for ease of navigation. This will be followed by the summary, but we address this section later in this chapter.

Background information

This part of the report reviews the individual's previous history and care will be required at every stage as this can include sensitive issues – the way they are approached sets the tone of the whole report. As in the rest of the report, be both clear and succinct. Chapter 5 discusses all the areas to investigate and from this a large amount of information will have been collected. It is neither necessary nor desirable to include all of it – sifting and summarising are required. Breaking the detail into appropriate sub-sections and providing headings will help to make it easier to read: the purpose of the assessment, developmental and medical history, educational history, current strengths and difficulties might be a suitable set of headings from which to work.

Always note the *purpose* of the assessment and clearly identify at whose request it was carried out. In the cases of children this will often be an observant teacher, but where parents have made the referral (perhaps because they are disappointed with the school's reaction to the problem), tact and diplomacy are required. Little will be gained by starting off with a statement such as *'His parents feel that Billy has been let down badly by the school and are desperate for advice'*, even if this is closer to the truth. For adults, the purpose could be described as *'an opportunity to gain a greater insight into his/her strengths and difficulties'*. There is a strong psychological impact of reading the words *greater*, *insight* and *strengths* (all positive concepts) before getting to the word *difficulties* (almost an afterthought).

Assessors must take a balanced approach to reporting developmental and medical information; greater detail is likely to be needed for young children than adults. In all cases, it is advisable to note that any hearing, vision or medical reasons for difficulties have been excluded. Similarly, the educational history section will establish if there have been adequate opportunities for learning and set out any issues if English is an additional language.

In reporting current difficulties, limit the detail to the main concerns – a report with every single difficultly listed over a page or two makes for depressing reading. Also, the more detail that is included, the shorter the 'life' of the report, as individual situations can change quite quickly. However, at times, perhaps particularly in cases where urgent action needs to be taken to support the individual, more detail will be appropriate.

Throughout, assessors must check that individuals are happy to see any sensitive personal, medical or educational detail included. For example, this might be the case if one of the parents has dyslexia, or if a child is facing difficulty at school because of family circumstances. Permission must be sought before such information is presented to the world. Young people and adults might not want some elements of their past chronicled in detail for future colleges or employers.

Test conditions

This brief section will note the setting of the assessment and exclude or note any external circumstances that might have influenced the result, such as illness, distractions, motivation, behaviour, or any test alterations, or use of a coloured overlay. Were the test conditions suitable such that the results represent a reliable estimate of the individual's skills and abilities?

The main body of the report

This part of the report discusses each test in turn and details the findings. We suggest that the following areas are addressed for each test, although the order and prominence of each part can be decided on an individual basis.

- **Test information** – test name? What skill was tested? How?
- **Quantitative data** – the scores, a description and possibly mention of the relationship to expected performance considering the age and stage of the individual.
- **Qualitative data** – the skills and strategies applied and test behaviour observed.
- **Analysis and impact** – what is the impact for the individual of any strengths and weaknesses found? Links to other parts of the evidence might be noted if appropriate.

Test information

As a starting point, it is helpful to explain the nature of the tests that have been used and to detail briefly what was required. It is important to describe the tests in plain English, as copying verbatim from the manual is often unhelpful.

Quantitative data: reporting scores

For each test undertaken, it is common practice to set out the test result and follow it with a commentary. We recommend a balanced approach to reporting statistical data, with the substantial bulk reserved for the technical appendix and only key pieces of information presented in the main body of the report. Consider the following description of a reading test result:

Matilda achieved a standard score in the WRAT4 (blue form) single-word reading test of 72, at the 3rd percentile, with a confidence interval of 65–81 at the 95% level, which is close to 2 standard deviations below the population mean. A statistically significant difference at the 0.01 level exists between this score and her sentence reading comprehension, with a prevalence rate of less than 5%.

This might be accurate but it is near impenetrable!

A better approach would be to leave out the detail and use more everyday terminology to describe the findings:

Matilda was able to read a range of straightforward words but multi-syllable words proved more difficult and her test score of 72 was well below average. This represents a substantial weakness in comparison to her sentence reading comprehension.

The professional who wants to explore the details should be able to do so in the technical appendix.

While we might usually start the test commentary by stating the score and its relationship to the average, depending on circumstances, there is certainly no need to do this on every occasion. The inclusion of explanatory and non-statistical adjectives might make for more agreeable reading and provide helpful information for the non-specialist:

'Jacob's score in this test showed that his reading comprehension skills are secure at average levels' is equally useful, more positive and perhaps more interesting than *'Jacob scored 105 in this test which falls in the average range.'*

Where scores are particularly low, especially in the sections reporting on attainment, it might be easier to begin with a comment on the approach to the task or a strategy employed:

'Harvey found this test challenging but he persevered and attempted all the words presented. He was able to spell some straightforward vocabulary, such as…. (give one or two examples), however, overall his score was below the level expected for his age.'

This replaces the utterly crushing: *'Harvey's spelling score of 70 was well below average; his score at the 2nd percentile indicates that 98% of individuals of his age would do better.'*

This example shows how a percentile score can cause harm. Similarly, an age-equivalent score could do serious damage. Imagine Harvey was 14 years old, but the score suggested he had a reading age of 7 years old. Does this information support him? **We strongly suggest age-equivalent scores are entirely avoided, with possible rare exceptions for the very young.**

Yet, even when scores are very low, there are times when straightforward reporting of scores will help the reader understand the profile. This might be especially the case when reporting diagnostic tests which expose underlying weaknesses. For example: *'Matilda's ability to work with the sounds in words was weak, revealed by a well below average score of 73 in the phonological awareness test. This is one diagnostic feature of her dyslexia and partly explains why she finds accurate reading and spelling difficult.'*

Celebrating average

For our purpose, average scores can be noted positively in every case and errors in the most advanced parts of the test (complex spellings, for example) need not be highlighted. This applies even where the score is lower than expected, given excellent underlying potential; individuals can be reassured that although they have some concerns their achievements are still just as good as the majority:

'Erin achieved a secure average score of 105 in this test. She was able to read a commendable range of vocabulary and her skills are equivalent to most people her age. However, her reading was not always fluent and given her excellent verbal abilities, her score is somewhat lower than anticipated – this is often the case for those with dyslexia.'

Finally in regard to reporting scores, a note must be made on reporting relative differences. In order to be positive and highlight strengths, particularly in cases of very weak profiles, it is sometimes tempting to overstate the role of relatively higher scores, but this must not set up false hope or rely on differences which are not substantial.

Take a comparison between a single-word reading score of 74 and a spelling score of 59. '*Jacob showed a relative strength in his single-word reading skills although his spelling was weak*', might lead some to assume his reading is fine. Instead, report weaknesses in both areas but note the strategies used and indicate that positive steps can be taken to help.

Qualitative data: reporting skills, strategies and test observations

The assessment observations will have provided valuable insights into how the individual tackles each task. Similarly, the coping strategies that the individual has developed will also have been noted. These snippets of information can be woven into the report – it gives an individual touch and will help future teachers gauge which strategies need development. For example, in spelling, is there reliance on sounding out or on visual strategies? Notes on test behaviour might also be needed. For example, if an individual asks to stop the test as soon as he is less than 100% certain of the answer, this reluctance to take risks is a valuable indicator of lack of confidence and would be worthy of inclusion, with readers directed to take account of this when interpreting the score.

The exception to this rule would be if the subject had confided that he felt 'stupid'. This word (or any other equally derogative term) should never appear in a report, even as a direct quotation. It is one thing for a vulnerable person to confess such a thing in the privacy of the assessment room; it is quite another to have it embedded in print. An assessor is in a position of trust and must be ever mindful of the responsibility that this entails.

Analysis and impact

Take care to analyse results and explain the impact of the findings in each test, or provide a summary at the end of each section (reading, writing, cognitive). It is a good idea to take the opportunity here to make links across tests and explain apparent anomalies. Why is it, for example, that Matilda has such difficulty with reading individual words, yet still achieves a good reading comprehension score? (It might be that she is able to make use of context and apply her wider knowledge successfully to predict words.)

Reporting cognitive abilities: underlying verbal and non-verbal abilities

Perhaps the most important thing in this section of the report is to approach conclusions and comments regarding 'intelligence' with extreme caution.

Reporting successful outcomes in these tests is straightforward. The phrase *'Emily has excellent logical reasoning skills and her knowledge and use of language are exceptional'* could be used. For many with SpLDs this could be the first time that they have been described as being excellent at anything. The same will be true if these abilities are found to be good or even at the expected standard for this age – here is a prime example of an opportunity to celebrate an average score: *'Emily has a range of competent abilities at average levels.'*

Clearly, there will be instances where these scores are not strong, but honest reporting is still required. How much kinder it is to say that scores fall *'below the anticipated standard'* than to use words such as *poor* or the dreadful *'intellectually impaired'* which appears in some test manuals. Younger children (up to about eight years) with low scores could be described as *'less well developed than is usual for his age'*, as there is a possibility that they may catch up.

Where subtest scores are in very strong contrast, and bearing in mind our statistical discussions in Chapter 2, we recommend assessors take an individual approach which reports and explains each component. For example: *'Chris performed well in three out of four of these tests of underlying ability; these results suggest ...'* and go on to describe the strengths and weaknesses without necessarily referring to composite scores, which might serve to obscure the detail of the assessment findings.

Sometimes the individual might feel embarrassed by his weaknesses – particularly in verbal abilities, which he feels should be secure. This is particularly true of older secondary students and adults. If this is the case, we can sometimes reassure them that extensive language is built partly via reading, and that it can be improved. Ideally, this reassurance will have been given in person at the assessment, and it would be helpful to include a reminder in the report.

Reporting cognitive processing abilities

Most people will not have come across terms like 'phonological' abilities or 'working memory' before reading the report. Assessors might want to explain that research has shown that these skills tend to be weak in individuals with SpLDs. Describe each area briefly and note its role in everyday tasks. Here is an example of reporting a rapid-naming test using everyday language which moves from test, to score, to impact – a useful formula to follow:

'Erin's ability to retrieve well-known information (such as letters, words and numbers) quickly from her long-term memory was weaker than expected and her score of 67 falls in the very low range. This difficulty partly explains why she finds she reads and writes more slowly than her peers; she knows many words but she cannot bring them to mind quickly.'

Reporting literacy and numeracy attainments

When analysing results of literacy or numeracy tests, be particularly mindful of the individual's sensitivities. This is often the part of the assessment report he dreads most!

It is far better to focus in a positive way on the strategies that have been used to tackle the tasks. A note can be made of which approaches and skills are being used effectively, partly or not at all. This will be immensely valuable for later teaching.

Do not adopt the negative approach of listing all the errors made (so demoralising!) and trying to categorise them. Phrases such as *'Ben used context to self-correct the word "conversion" (originally read as "conversation") or 'Amy used her knowledge of sound and common word endings to spell "physician" ("fizition")'* are positive approaches to the issue of errors. This approach is also more succinct, as just one or two errors can be produced to illustrate each observed strategy. A very detailed analysis might be supplied to a specialist teacher later, but it does not need to appear in the report.

When reporting on writing, a positive comment is always welcome, even if it was *'he made a good start'* or *'the ideas were interesting and the writing shows potential for development'*. There is no need to comment on every aspect, and certainly not on every error. Key themes should be highlighted: content, legibility, structure, grammar and punctuation and spelling. What is appropriate will vary greatly, but here is one example to give a flavour:

'After some discussion and encouragement, Ben chose to write about his interests, including the recent computer games he had enjoyed. He wrote for 20 minutes and was able to communicate a good knowledge of his favourite games. His handwriting was easily legible. He wrote in a logical, straightforward way but there were inaccuracies in basic punctuation and quite a high number of spelling errors.'

Summaries and conclusions

While the summary appears at the beginning of the report, we have chosen to discuss these two sections together to explore more easily the differences between them. The **summary** provides information about all the key aspects of the assessment, from referral to recommendation. The **conclusion**, however, is where the assessor tells the story of how the diagnostic decision was reached; it is the written equivalent of a face-to-face feedback session. The following thematic structures are offered simply as a tool to be used flexibly for each section and can be adapted as professionals develop their own style.

Summaries

In the summary we suggest the assessor reports on the reasons for referral, the main findings, the diagnostic decision and the main recommendations; headings are optional. Here is a sample summary in a case of dyslexia. Note the absence of test names and scores; this technical and detailed information will be reported elsewhere.

Reason for Referral	This assessment was undertaken to explore Jonathan's strengths and difficulties in relation to accessing the school curriculum. Jonathan's teachers are concerned that he might have a specific learning difficulty and they wished to know how he might be best supported.
Main Findings: Cognitive Abilities	The assessment revealed that Jonathan's underlying abilities are secure, indicating good potential for learning. In contrast, he has weaknesses in working memory, the ability to manipulate information in the mind, and in phonological awareness, the awareness of the sound structure of language which underpins efficient literacy skills. These are diagnostic features of dyslexia.
Main Findings: Impact on Jonathan/ Strengths and weaknesses	These weaknesses have an impact on Jonathan in school activities. He faces difficulties in reading accurately and at speed, his spelling is weaker than expected and his handwriting is slow and difficult to decipher. He also finds it difficult to organise his ideas in writing. However, it must also be noted that Jonathan is a creative and expressive writer. He has excellent spoken language skills, and has developed good strategies to support his reading comprehension.
Diagnostic Decision	The evidence from the assessment shows that Jonathan has a profile of dyslexia.
Main Recommendations	Jonathan will benefit from strategies to support him in the classroom and a series of specialist teaching sessions. He will find it helpful to be introduced to some IT-based study aids. He should also be considered for examination access arrangements. Further information is given in the 'Recommendations' section at the end of this report.

Conclusions

By contrast, the conclusion would not normally include the referral or the recommendations, but instead focus on the reason the diagnostic decision has been reached.

If a conclusion is drawn that there is sufficient weight of evidence to warrant note of a co-occurring difficulty, it is useful to add some explanation so that individuals do not go away thinking they have two (or in some cases multiple) disabilities. For example, if the conclusion is drawn that both dyslexia and dyspraxia are evident, we could say: *'It is very common for these characteristics to co-exist and overlap. This does not mean that Jacob has two disabilities, simply that he has a unique profile which does not neatly fit into one category.'*

There are also likely to be occasions when there seems to be so much overlap, or the profile so unusual, that we might instead use the label 'specific learning difficulty' for the final conclusion. We would go on to describe the key features and impact of the profile and again offer reassurance that variation in profiles is common.

Diagnostic Decision	Taking all the evidence of the assessment into account, Jonathan's profile of skills, abilities and characteristics confirms that he has dyslexia. While Jonathan has a range of strengths, he has unexpected weaknesses in his information processing abilities which are key diagnostic features of dyslexia.
Underlying Cognitive Abilities	Jonathan has excellent spoken language skills and his teachers report that he contributes in an articulate way to class discussions. He has a wide vocabulary, his verbal reasoning skills are above average, and he has secure logical thinking and problem-solving skills. These results show that he has good potential for learning and his abilities will support him well in the future.
Cognitive Processing Abilities: Weaknesses and their impact on the classroom.	However, in sharp contrast, Jonathan has underlying difficulties with processing information, which are characteristic of dyslexia. He finds it hard to identify and work with the sounds of words. This makes it more difficult for him to read and spell words accurately. He also finds he is unable to bring information quickly to mind – even when he knows it well – and is slower than expected to retrieve words. This has an impact on his reading and writing speeds. A further difficulty is seen in his working memory, which is a common feature of dyslexia. Jonathan cannot easily hold onto a lot of information in his mind. This affects many areas of study, but it is seen for example in the difficulties Jonathan described in reading comprehension, where he has to re-read several times to absorb information, in his struggle to copy accurately from the board, and in his difficulties with the organisation of ideas.
Summary: Literacy Weaknesses	These difficulties mean that Jonathan's reading accuracy, comprehension and speed are below average, his spelling skills are weak and his written composition skills are less fluent and effective than expected.
Summary: Strengths	Despite these difficulties Jonathan has still been able to demonstrate very creative skills in writing – he has plenty of ideas and can produce imaginative and original stories. He is also able to use his wide knowledge of language to help him in reading. In addition, he has a passion for maths and science and he has done well in these subjects in school.
Next Steps	To help Jonathan make more confident progress, ideas for adjustments and support follow in the recommendations section below.

In cases where there is insufficient evidence to conclude that SpLDs exist, a variation on the following will be needed, so there is no doubt: *'While there are some contrasts in Jenny's profile of scores, they are not unusual within the general population and do not indicate the presence of a specific learning difficulty.'*

This can feel more difficult where reported difficulties are not at their heart caused by a *specific* issue, but as a result of overall low ability. Here, as above, it remains important to be clear, but at the same time to be as positive and encouraging as possible. *'The assessment results do not reveal a specific learning difficulty. John faced significant challenges across a broad range of these assessments and he will need ongoing support to develop his skills.'*

Recommendations

The conclusion is followed by the recommendations: individualised, precise and clearly structured, addressing current and future needs, as appropriate.

A clear but measured tone is needed, taking a view of what is reasonable. It is no good indicating that the only way forward is one-to-one specialist teaching for three hours a week if this is utterly impractical. An assessor might recommend such an approach, but avoid suggesting all will be lost if this is not undertaken. Caution must also apply because it is rarely possible to guarantee that recommendations are carried out – unless perhaps assessors are to deliver a subsequent teaching programme themselves. On the other hand, clearly stated needs can help individuals to secure appropriate resources.

As throughout, tact and diplomacy are needed when writing recommendations; if they are perceived as criticisms of current provision by 'someone from outside' they might do more harm than good. Therefore, when suggesting a programme, try to recognise and build on what good practice already exists. Emails are wonderful but, especially in sensitive circumstances, they are no substitute for making personal contact.

Closing the report

To close the report, assurances can be given that the assessor is happy to respond to any subsequent questions. Then, finally, an encouraging comment, as appropriate, is a good way to finish, perhaps wishing him success in his goals, or reassuring him he can make progress, or even a note that it was a pleasure to meet and work with him.

Technical appendix

The technical appendix follows and is the perfect place for all the detailed statistical data which formed part of the underpinning analysis, but which would otherwise weigh down the main body of the report. It is included chiefly to enable the professional reader to track carefully through the analysis and see, at a glance, all of the quantitative data on which the conclusion relies. However, it must remain accessible to all report readers, therefore give explanations of technical terms.

The details to include are as follows:

Test information: Give the full publication reference (author, date of publication, full title, edition, test form, etc) so that any future assessor has precise knowledge of materials used. Only include tests that were actually employed, in order to avoid suspicion that a section of comment has been missed.

Scores: Of course the scores achieved in the assessment must be reported here. A table is recommended, as it is easier to read. Score descriptors should be reported and the approach adopted explained.

Confidence intervals and other statistical measures: If all the statistical information does not easily fit into a table, additional text or footnotes could be used to describe statistical significance issues or prevalence rates. For example:

'The composite verbal and visual ability scores have not been reported because statistically significant differences at the 95% confidence level were evident.'

Visual display

Including a graph of scores is an option and it can be very helpful in giving a non-specialist an overview. We recommend a standard score rather than percentile scale – given the latter's tendency to misrepresent the size of score discrepancies. And consideration must be given to how key data which is not standardised – perhaps a reading speed – is to be included.

Summary

- The most important reader of the report is the individual himself, and concern for his best interests must be at the heart of the approach. However, as different audiences are likely to read the report, their needs must be considered.
- The language chosen must be accessible to the non-specialist reader, but adopt a professional and informed tone, with a sensitive and positive, yet clear and honest approach.
- The report must be accurate – in terms of scores, analysis and presentation. Errors in one part raise questions about the accuracy of the remainder.
- Assessors are recommended to follow a clearly structured format.
- Descriptions of scores and statistical data can be kept to a minimum and supported with non-statistical language. The bulk of statistical data should be given in the technical appendix.
- Qualitative analysis of performance is equally as important as scores. This should include comment on skills and strategies employed, and the impact of any difficulties.
- Lists of errors are to be avoided; note strengths.
- Recommendations should be individual, reasonable, achievable, tactful and easy to navigate.

PART THREE

Through the Age Range

10 The Early Years

In England, the statutory framework of the Early Years Foundation Stage (EYFS)[1] aims to strengthen the partnership between parents and professionals to give children a secure start to their education. This partnership holds the key to the early identification of children who might be at risk of dyslexia or other specific learning difficulties.

Particular considerations for assessment in the early years

A major concern for practitioners in the early years is in knowing which of children's observable behaviours are developmental and which signal potential SpLDs. All children develop at their own unique rate and comparisons between individual children are not helpful in determining which children might be at risk.

The EYFS framework calls for a progress check at age 2 and further assessment against early learning goals at age 5. The resulting profile is shared with the Year 1 teacher, although it is not intended as a screening tool for SpLD. Therefore, while these assessments provide useful information, continuous assessment and observation is also a key part of early years' practice.

This careful observation will help determine whether individual children have needs which warrant additional resources or support. These observations, accumulated over time, should be supplemented by parents, nursery staff, other early years' practitioners and by the children themselves.

Early indicators of 'at risk' characteristics

Practitioners will be aware that home circumstances and environmental factors differ widely and for many young children simply starting nursery or reception can be a daunting experience. The key is to observe children who do not conform to the usual expectations for the Foundation Stage, with the aim of collecting detailed information to support possible future identification of an SpLD or need for intervention. Specific concerns in communication, phonology, memory, alphabet knowledge, motor coordination or attention might contribute to a picture where children are considered 'at risk'. It will be useful for practitioners to note relevant findings and observations in these areas.

---

[1] Statutory Framework for the Early Years Foundation Stage (EYFS) www.education.gov.uk/schools/teachingandlearning/curriculum/a0068102/early-years-foundation-stage-eyfs

In all cases, information from parents will provide additional background. Any concerns they have should be considered. They will be able to give a picture of their child outside the school which might be illuminating. Also, given the heritable nature of SpLD, if concerns emerge, it might be useful to seek information tactfully about any history of specific difficulties in the family.

Action: note down…
- information on siblings/family members who had problems acquiring literacy skills.

Speech, language and vocabulary

We see an increasing proportion of children beginning school with poor speech and language skills. However, if parents report very scant, indistinct or poor speech, advice might be sought from speech and language professionals. If English is an additional language, it might be helpful to ask if this pattern is evident in the language spoken at home.

We know how crucial oral language ability is for the development of written language. Children who have poor spoken language skills at the Foundation Stage are more likely to have problems acquiring the literacy skills they need in Key Stage 1 and beyond. Within the context of the Foundation Stage Profile, practitioners will monitor children's language acquisition and if difficulties are observed, examples can usefully be noted.

Action: note down…
- family information concerning late development of speech;
- references to non-family members finding it hard to understand the child;
- references to the child being later than others in attaching names to everyday objects or colours;
- examples of substituted 'near miss' words – e.g. *lamp post* for *lampshade*; *water pot* for *watering can*;
- examples of persistent jumbled phrases and spoonerisms like *beddy tear* for *teddy bear* and *par cark* for *car park*;
- bizarre forms of words, such as *suebegi* for *spaghetti*, *plisters* for *slippers*, where the listener cannot identify the correct target word.

The Early Years Statutory Framework places high emphasis on children having opportunities to experience a rich language environment to develop their confidence and skills in expressing themselves and to speak and listen in a range of situations. The average 3 year old should have a vocabulary of over 1000 words, which rapidly increases, such that a 5 year old should have an expressive vocabulary of over 2000 words and a receptive vocabulary of substantially more.

In addition, the average 5 year old should be able to:

- repeat a sentence of twelve syllables, e.g. *'I'm going to play in the park with my friend'*;
- give four objects in order: *'Bring me your coat, scarf, hat and boots'*;
- understand *What*, *Where*, *Who*, *When* and *Why* questions;
- use a sentence of more than five words in length.

Yet some children who have SpLDs might have problems with vocabulary, and word-finding in particular, and this could be apparent even at the Foundation Stage. Children might take an inordinately long time to communicate their meaning and use gesture to accompany their speech. Or they might frequently have their hand up during circle time, or 'show and tell', but have forgotten what they wanted to say when invited to respond. Individually such factors might not seem significant, but when put into a wider picture, they can contribute to a profile of possible specific difficulties.

Action: note down children who...

- have word-finding difficulties;
- have their hands up but cannot answer appropriately;
- attach the incorrect verbal labels to everyday items;
- use gesture, pointing or mime to convey meaning, more than other children do.

Phonological abilities

There is a crucial link between phonological abilities and learning to read and spell, therefore weaknesses here are a strong 'at risk' indicator. Foundation Stage children should be able to recite nursery rhymes and to join in with them, supplying the missing rhymes, thus *'Jack and Jill went up the ....'*. By 5 years old most children should be able to give rhyming words; they might be asked for words or non-words to match a given target. They will also be able to isolate initial sounds. To investigate, they might be asked to give words beginning with a particular letter, or play games which require judgements on the basis of 'odd man out' – where three out of four objects begin with the same initial sound, for example ' pencil, pin, *scissors*, paintbrush.'

Action: take careful note if a child is unable to do any of the following:

- recite a nursery rhyme;
- identify the odd man out in sequences like *cat/pig/bat/mat*;
- generate rhymes: *cat/fat/mat/ ?... (hat, sat, pat)*;
- classify words or objects on the basis of the first phoneme (alliteration);
- provide inaccurate responses when playing I-Spy, because he has not understood that it is the first phoneme which is required to guess the target word.

If weaknesses are observed, any training or enrichment activities that help children to develop their phonological abilities will be of benefit.

There are many resources available to support both assessment and teaching of phonological abilities.[2]

Verbal short-term and working memory

Reliably assessing the speed and efficacy of memory abilities in very young children is not easy. However, practitioners can note children who have more difficulty than their peers in a range of activities making demands on memory.

For example, in the EYFS Framework, under **'listening and attention'** goals, children are expected to:

- listen to stories, accurately anticipate key events and respond to what they hear with relevant comments, questions or actions;
- give their attention to what others say and respond appropriately, while engaged in another activity;
- follow instructions involving several ideas or actions.

In **number** work, they are also expected to:

- count reliably with numbers from 1 to 20, place them in order and say which number is one more or one less than a given number;
- using quantities and objects, add and subtract two single-digit numbers and count on or back to find the answer;
- solve problems, including doubling, halving and sharing.

Useful observations can be made beyond these areas. It is helpful to note the child who, when following a set of procedures, suddenly forgets what to do next, or the child who is observed in PE to be several seconds behind his peers in his responses, often because he is watching other children to see what to do next, since he cannot remember or interpret the teacher's oral instructions.

Action: note down children who...

- cannot retell a simple story they have just heard;
- cannot repeat a four-item sequence or set of actions;
- have difficulty using numbers as labels;
- have great difficulty in sequencing a set of three picture cards in correct order;
- are unable to play 'my aunt went to market and bought....'
- fail to remember class jingles, routines and chants.

---

[2] For example see Backhouse, G. and Ruback, P. (2011) *Special Needs Language and Literacy Assessment Handbook,* Hodder Education.

Alphabet knowledge, reading and writing

Research has shown that secure alphabet knowledge is the single, strongest predictor of later reading proficiency. Early years practitioners will have a vast repertoire of activities to teach sound-symbol correspondence and to practise letter formation and identification. If, despite specific and structured teaching, children cannot associate letters with their correct sounds, or cannot reliably identify both upper and lower case letters by the end of the reception year, this would suggest another at risk indicator.

Action: note down children who, by the end of reception…
- cannot write their own full name correctly;
- cannot correctly identify 26 lower-case letters of the alphabet;
- have difficulty identifying the 26 upper-case letters;
- cannot sequence the alphabet orally and with plastic letters.

Looking beyond alphabet knowledge, the EYFS Framework expects a 5 year old to achieve the following literacy targets in reading and writing.

> *Reading: read and understand simple sentences; use phonic knowledge to decode regular words and read them aloud accurately; read some common irregular words; demonstrate understanding when talking with others about what they have read.*

> *Writing: use phonic knowledge to write words in ways which match their spoken sounds; write some irregular common words; write simple sentences which can be read by themselves and others; spell some words correctly and write others in a phonetically plausible way.*

Difficulties in these areas could possibly be the result of underlying cognitive difficulties, although of course a whole range of other factors would also have to be considered.

There are equivalent early learning goals for mathematics, including targets for sequencing and calculating numbers, and solving problems in the areas of shape, space and measurement. Assessment of these areas may also point to possible difficulties with language use, memory, sequencing and visual-spatial abilities.

Attention and perseverance

Children in the Foundation Stage should be able to sustain concentration, but practitioners might observe children who perform poorly on the listening and attention goals, who cannot concentrate during story time, who wander from one activity to another without any sustained engagement and who become overly frustrated or anxious when they cannot derive immediate success. Such children may also shun literacy-based activities. They might be finding it difficult to complete tasks because of limitations in attention and memory, or have possible language problems, although again, other factors will also be considered.

Action: note children who...

- are unable to sustain concentration (e.g. during story time);
- consistently avoid reading and writing-type activities;
- fail to persevere with table activities, so do not complete the task;
- seem to wander from one activity area to another, with minimal engagement;
- find it hard to play collaboratively (e.g. in the roleplay area or with outside equipment).

Motor coordination

The aim is for children to be active and interactive and to develop their coordination, control, and movement. Parents might report difficulties with early motor tasks and professionals might observe that children find both fine and gross motor activities challenging. Children who have very persistent difficulties in these areas might need further referral to child development teams – perhaps a physiotherapist. In any case, where weaknesses are observed, extra opportunities for development will of course be useful.

Action: note children who...

- show poor control and coordination in large and small movements;
- do not move confidently and find negotiating space difficult;
- have difficulty handling equipment and tools effectively, including pencils for writing.

Reaching conclusions

At this stage it is difficult to make any definitive conclusions about children who might have specific learning difficulties. One risk factor alone does not constitute dyslexia or other SpLD profile. Some children grow out of their problems, and there could be a host of other causal factors, such as otitis media (glue-ear), which might have delayed some aspects of cognitive development, or family, social, emotional or environmental factors.

It must also be remembered that some children within the Foundation Stage who exhibit *none* of the risk factors discussed above, will later go on to be assessed as having a specific learning difficulty. Such children may begin school with no apparent difficulties or mask them very successfully. Their specific problems with literacy only manifest later when curriculum demands increase.

Summary

- observe closely and record carefully;
- where a number of risk factors emerge, a collaborative approach with parents and colleagues will be the most useful way forward. A picture of the strengths and weaknesses of the child can be built to inform early intervention;
- further referrals to other professionals might be necessary.

11 The Primary Phase

We have seen in the previous chapter how information gathered in the Foundation Stage can identify the 'at risk' child. This monitoring process will continue through the statutory assessment at age 5, the Year 1 phonics screening check, the Year 2 teacher assessments and all the ongoing monitoring through Key Stages 1 and 2. Early identification of specific difficulties during the primary stage is a key goal.

Particular considerations for the primary age range

A huge learning curve takes place during the primary phase of education. By the time a child leaves primary school he is expected to have mastered functional and fluent literacy skills. Children who have not reached this stage face the daunting prospect of entering secondary school knowing that they have already fallen behind their peers and may be unable to access the secondary curriculum. These are the children who often learn in a different way and individual assessment can identify the additional support they need. It is possible to make a significant difference by appropriate interventions to improve literacy and maths skills, and develop effective learning strategies.

Children who learn differently

David *(age 7 years 3 months)*

David is struggling to develop more than a basic sight vocabulary, but he uses context well in reading. He has found it hard to learn his individual letter sounds and is reluctant to write more than one sentence. His mother reports that he was slow learning to speak. When he did, his speech was full of mispronunciations, especially with polysyllabic words. This difficulty is still obvious as he struggles to say *capital letters* and *consonants*, which he pronounces as *catipal* letters and *consternants*. Any suggestion that he has general language difficulties is belied by his good comprehension and verbosity. But when he tells his news, his speech is circumlocutory and full of *'whatchammacallits'* as he struggles to express himself clearly and access the words he needs. Sometimes the names he uses demonstrate a clear image being accessed rather than a verbal label: for example, he talks about a *camera-picture* rather than a photograph; a *flat* egg rather than a fried one. His mother reports that he found nursery rhymes difficult to remember, although if they were sung he could recall them more efficiently. She also noted that he was poor at carrying out instructions. If told to go upstairs, put on his pyjamas and clean his teeth, he would remember to do one only. Yet he appears to be much better than his friends at building Lego models and is a keen footballer. She is very concerned, as his father was identified as having dyslexia as an adult.

Joanna (age 9 years 7 months)

Joanna is reluctant to write. She is unhappy about her handwriting, which is large and untidy. Her pencil grip is awkward – she uses four fingers rather than the traditional tripod grip. She produces far less written work than her peers, although she has excellent ideas for stories and a wide vocabulary when speaking. She likes reading and enjoys drama. She finds it hard to structure her writing, which tends to be disorganised. She sticks with 'safe to spell' words, yet still makes spelling mistakes, often in the visual recall of letter patterns.

Joanna also experiences difficulties with maths: she has problems with place value beyond three digits. She does not know her tables and rarely contributes in mental maths sessions. Her untidiness and poor layout in written work add to her difficulties.

School staff have noted these difficulties, as well as her general tendency to be untidy and fidgety. They concede that she might not be reaching her potential, but do not see a major problem. Her parents, however, are most anxious about the fact that Joanna is unhappy at school and, in particular, dislikes games and PE.

Individuals like David and Joanna are noticeable in class as being different from other children; they are also very different from each other. Specific learning difficulties have many guises. Some children will be easy to identify very early as they struggle to learn alphabet sounds. Others will cope with the early stages of reading through developing a good sight vocabulary, although they might never manage to crack the alphabetic code completely. Others might not be noticed until their difficulties with spelling and writing to an age-appropriate standard emerge.

Assessment at primary level

Background information and observation

A comprehensive picture of the child is needed at the primary stage drawn from information provided by parents and teachers. Parents are the people who know their children best and become worried if they do not make the same progress as peers or older siblings: their concerns should always be heeded. Anxiety frequently accompanies difficulties at school and shows itself in an unwillingness to get ready in the morning, tummy aches and 'clamming up' about the school day. Parents will also be the best source of information on early motor and language development, and such information is crucial.

In primary school, children are predominantly allocated one class teacher who will be aware of the child who is not learning as expected. She has often had experience of hundreds of children passing through this phase of education, so is a hugely important source of information. The classroom assistant also works closely with individual children and may have a very useful contribution to make.

The development of spoken language is always a key area to observe. Does the child express himself easily and fluently, or are there immaturities or difficulties in articulation (e.g. *lellow* instead of *yellow*) or in use of language (e.g. *Miss telled me*)? There may be a tendency to interpret words literally, for example *'You need to pull your socks up.'*

Having gathered this information before the assessment, informal questioning of the child himself during the assessment will add even more to this growing picture. Does he like reading and writing? What does he read? What does he enjoy most at school? What does he think he is good at? What, if anything, does he dislike? What would he like more help with? The ensuing conversation can be very illuminating and will tell much about the child's self-esteem and how his difficulties have been managed in the school setting. A child with weak reading skills might report he loves reading. This will be a child who has been handled sensitively, who has read books that were manageable, and therefore enjoyable.

Cognitive abilities

It is important to explore both the verbal and non-verbal domains of **underlying ability**. Weak vocabulary underpins many pupils' difficulties with reading and comprehension, thus it is vital this is investigated in some detail – for both expressive and receptive language skills.

If verbal abilities are significantly low alongside weak comprehension and grammatical skills, a specific language impairment might be suspected. In this case referral to a Speech and Language Therapist would be appropriate. However, it is also important to note any strengths in nonverbal ability.

The primary classroom makes many demands on both **working memory** and rote learning. For example, an efficient working memory is required for sound blending, mental arithmetic, compositional writing and following complex verbal instructions or explanations. This can be assessed formally. Informal assessment would identify difficulties with rote learning such as is required for learning common sequences.

As **phonological skills** underpin literacy skills, this is a vital area to assess. A careful, step-by-step analysis through the stages of phonological awareness development will investigate if he can work with syllables, make use of rhyme, and manipulate phonemes. Observe if skills are automatic and fluent. Many well-structured resources are available to identify problems and train these skills.[1] Any work in this area should be oral/aural, not written. Other tasks will address the child's *phonic* knowledge and skills.

Assessors will also test any difficulties in his speed of accessing and retrieving words – both through formal rapid-naming tests, and also through observation and interaction throughout the assessment process. Primary assessors might also

---

[1] For example, see Backhouse, G. and Ruback, P. (2011) *Special Needs Language and Literacy Assessment Handbook,* Hodder Education.

consider if there is a contrast between phonological and semantic fluency. For example, a pupil with dyslexia might show a relative weakness in the phonological task, where the pupil with general difficulties, or English as Additional Language, will find accessing words by meaning equally as difficult as accessing them by sound.

Attainments

Sound-symbol correspondence

Testing sound-symbol correspondence is recommended at this age range. It should not be taken for granted that it has been fully mastered. This can be assessed using tactile letters in the early stages. Confusion between letter names and sounds is a common cause of spelling errors.

Reading

Tests in this area would include single-word recognition, speed of word reading, non-word reading and lists of high-frequency irregular words from the relevant Year and Key Stage. These will give a detailed knowledge of the child's relative use of decoding skills and sight-word recognition, which is particularly important in planning teaching. How far does he have knowledge of alphabetic principles? Does he recognise initial letters but guess medial and final sounds? Does he rely on the shape and appearance of words?

Tests of reading comprehension and fluency are also needed to observe the child's reading strategies. In what ways does he approach text? Does he take cues from context or pictures? Does he self-correct? Miscue analysis (see page 173) will provide additional quantified evidence of reading strategies. Are there any signs of visual discomfort or tracking difficulties, for example omitting words or skipping/repeating lines? Is the reader able to make inferences or is he only successful when asked for literal responses, or is he adept at simply 'lifting' the appropriate text for the answer? (This might suggest an underlying comprehension problem masked by good sight-word and contextual strategies.)

Reading accuracy and comprehension scores should be compared and substantial differences noted and explored. Children with dyslexia might read single words inaccurately but still achieve good comprehension scores, using context clues or other general knowledge to help them. If comprehension is lower than accuracy, it might be that the effort of decoding prevents meaning being fully accessed, or other language difficulties exist. In either case, it can be useful to re-run the test using a parallel set of passages purely as a listening comprehension activity.

Spelling

Spelling skills should be analysed in both single words and in a piece of unaided free writing. Formal spelling tests will provide both quantitative and qualitative data and might be supplemented by lists of key words appropriate for the Year and the Key Stage. Close observation of the *process* of creating written work will give an idea of how automated spelling patterns have become. A lack of automated spelling skills could be seen in frequent crossings-out and the use of 'safe to spell' vocabulary, often resulting in written work that does not match the level of expressive language.

It is particularly important at the primary stage to analyse spelling in the light of normal development patterns (see Chapter 1 for an introduction). Initially, there is no attempt to follow the order of speech sounds and a child may attempt to spell words by remembering how they look (*jmudpe* for *jumped* with an 'e' added as the word did not look long enough!) As more speech sounds are identified, he moves forward to *jpt, jupt,* and ultimately *jumpt*. Finally, *jumped* indicates that the child understands the significance of the past-tense marker *-ed* and is able to integrate the various contributing skills needed for spelling. Alphabetic spelling of high-frequency irregular words such as *sed/said, wos/was* are common at this stage, and should be seen in a positive light initially.

When looking diagnostically at spelling skills and strategies, note the level of phonic knowledge revealed: single letters, blends, digraphs, common letter strings (e.g. *-tion*). Are there sounds in words for which the child has no phonic representation? For example, does he write *lok* instead of *look* (oo), *bening* instead of *burning* (ur), *crach* instead of *crash* (sh)? Are errors phonetic, semi-phonetic or sometimes bizarre (e.g. *kerm* rather than *garden*)? Does the child vocalise whilst sounding out spellings, or is he quick and confident? Are common irregular words spelled correctly, or are the correct letters present but in the wrong order? Is he displaying knowledge of spelling rules?

Free writing

In analysing writing, as well as the obvious more technical skills of spelling, grammar, use of punctuation, clarity of handwriting and writing speed, do consider content, vocabulary, style and structure. There is sometimes evidence of creativity in the work of a child whose writing and spelling are almost undecipherable. Do not forget to look out for and acknowledge this almost buried talent – it needs to be encouraged. Also consider if the child is able to sustain focus on writing, or whether his approach is rushed and apparently careless.

When looking at handwriting, consider handedness, letter formation/proportion, letter and word spacing, style (cursive/print/mixed), pencil grip/control and paper position, as well as body position/posture. Information on the handwriting policy of the school will be helpful. Look for difficulties with letter/number orientation, particularly *b/d, p/q, 9/p* or the use of capitalised versions of *B* and *D*. This is more significant after the age of seven, as these behaviours are common in the younger child. Is there any evidence of other fine motor skill difficulties?

Numeracy

Where significant weakness in numeracy skill has also been observed, testing of arithmetic and mathematical reasoning skills is recommended. There is a greater availability of tests of arithmetic than mathematical reasoning and it will perhaps be necessary for assessors to devise investigations of their own. For very weak readers, tests should be administered orally.

Does the child understand how to count a number of things? Does he count on his fingers? Does he confuse number words, for example 16 with 60, or reverse numbers when he writes them down? Does he have a clear number line in his mind and can he see number patterns? Does he show signs of poor rote memory or working memory skills? What strategies are used for calculating? Does he confuse operational signs? Are there basic concepts he has not grasped? Can he estimate? Does he misinterpret maths language? Are there difficulties with layout and recording? Is he impulsive or considered in making responses?

Other areas of learning and development

Motor coordination

It is important to investigate any poor coordination affecting sport and activities such as riding a bicycle, bad posture, untidiness in the classroom, slowness or difficulty when changing for PE, slow and/or untidy writing, awkward pencil grip, and difficulties in practical activities. Referral to an occupational therapist/physiotherapist might be necessary.

Visual skills

Any visual difficulties need to be investigated. These problems may present as visual stress (print moving, eye fatigue, or weak tracking), or weak visual perception (the brain failing to make sufficient sense of what the eye sees). There may also be a problem with visual acuity. These difficulties would impact on reading, copying skills, spatial maths and interpreting diagrams and graphs.

Many pupils learn to use the mediating route of language to talk through what they need to analyse visually, so it is important to note the strategies used in tests, such as the non-verbal ability tests. Formal tests of visual motor integration as well as tests separating visual perception and motor skill are available and might help to isolate the source of difficulties.

Organisation

Organisational skills may be informally investigated through observation and questioning. The child might have difficulties with keeping personal possessions in order, getting started on activities, following the school timetable, or finding his way around school. Strategies for resolving these practical difficulties, which often cause a disproportionate amount of anxiety and irritation, should be suggested, working in partnership with parents and school staff.

Attention

A child's attention skills are developmental and underpin listening, concentration and memory. Immaturities in attention can be observed. Is he constantly fidgeting? Is it hard to get him to respond? In what situations do any difficulties occur? What other environmental factors might explain them?

Intervention and recommendations

Having identified the pupil's strengths and weaknesses and formulated conclusions, the next step is to address the difficulties. This might be through further referral – see Chapter 7 – or more commonly through a programme of teaching support. This can be done on several levels: individual support, group support and inclusion strategies devised for the classroom.

Specialist teaching on a one-to-one basis can be specifically designed to address a child's needs using a multisensory, structured, cumulative and sequential programme of work. There are many guides to specialist teaching intervention which provide detailed recommendations. The over-arching principle must be to engage the child in enjoyable learning, and to prepare him sufficiently for secondary school. Remediation needs to be considered alongside the development of coping strategies and use of technological compensatory tools.

Reading

To encourage text-level skills, regular access to books and reading material is needed. Paired reading[2], repeated reading, listening to stories and audio books will help to develop fluency and vocabulary. Books for independent reading should be at the correct level (i.e. where the child can achieve 95% accuracy), with a high interest factor. Discussing the content with another person will prove helpful from the earliest stages.

Automatic recognition of key words is an essential part of reading fluency in the early years, but these words are often irregular and carry little meaning out of context. Such words need to be embedded in sentences to enable the child to recall them. Games are essential here for over-learning.

Spelling

Phonological awareness and phonic knowledge underpin the ability to spell logically. If the pupil has serious phonological difficulties and is introduced to a structured spelling scheme too early, he is likely to use the visual similarities in words, but not relate them to the sounds.

Pupils with dyslexia finding it difficult to isolate phonemes, could be taught phonics though an analogy route using rime. There are many published programmes that work at the phoneme level. Irregular words can be taught using other strategies, such as mnemonics or visualisation.

---

[2] Paired reading is where a learner and a skilled reader share the reading of a text aloud. The precise approach will depend on the confidence and skill level of the learner. For example, the text might be read simultaneously, or alternative sentences read by each, or the learner might take over alone in some sections when confident, with the skilled reader supplying any unknown words.

Writing

It is important to address both the secretarial and compositional aspects of writing. Weak secretarial skills may be addressed by the recommendation of fine motor exercises, pencil grips, touch typing, or published resources to address punctuation and grammar. Compositional aspects involve structure, style and creativity. Storyboards, writing frames, mind maps, speech-activated software or a scribe provide a variety of options for support at the text level. This support will enable the child to enjoy the writing process.

Numeracy

The main recommendation for this age group would be the use of concrete materials to introduce and reinforce concepts and mathematical language, before they are abstracted into symbolic representations. Visual imagery linked to real-life situations can help a child talk through a problem or understand a concept. A maths reference book, containing a glossary of maths vocabulary and 'worked' examples with written explanations, could be created as individualised teaching is undertaken.

Outcomes of assessment: two case studies

David and Joanna were introduced earlier in this chapter. Let us now look at the way the evidence from the test results was used to draw conclusions about the nature of their difficulties.

David *(7 years 3 months)*

Standard Deviation		-3	-2	-1	0	+1	+2	+3
Standard Score		69–	70–84	85–89	90–110	111–115	116–130	131+
				Broad average range				
Tests: Cognitive Abilities								
Verbal ability							118	
Non-verbal ability						114		
Working memory			77					
Visual processing speed			81					
Phonological Awareness			76					
Phonological short-term memory				85				
Rapid automatic naming			83					
Tests: Attainments								
Reading accuracy – single word			72					
Reading comprehension (untimed)					90			
Sight-word reading (timed)			70					
Non-word reading (timed)		67						
Spelling – single word			79					
Basic number skills					100			

This layout is limited to standard scores only for the purposes of presenting a brief case study; assessors will wish to adapt their own score presentation style to include further test and technical detail (see Chapter 8).

David has a range of low scores in his cognitive processing abilities and literacy attainments. There is clear evidence of underlying phonological awareness and phonological processing difficulties. Working memory and visual processing speed are also weak. The assessment findings support the opinions of David's parents and his teacher that he is a boy of strong ability, as he has above-average scores in the verbal tests and high average scores in the non-verbal tests of underling ability. Taken together, the evidence indicates David has a profile of dyslexia.

The recommendations for a programme of support included combining oral rhyming games with a structured spelling programme, working at the onset and rime level to begin with. The need to use multisensory methods and to work on one regular pattern at a time, with just two or three high-frequency irregular words was emphasised. David's parents were taught paired reading techniques and agreed to read with him every day using this method.

Joanna *(9 years 7 months)*

Standard Deviation	−3	−2	−1	0	+1	+2	+3
Standard Score	69−	70–84	85–89	90–110	111–115	116–130	131+
				Broad average range			
Tests: Cognitive Abilities							
Verbal ability					113		
Non-verbal ability		84					
Working memory			87				
Visual processing speed	68						
Phonological awareness				109			
Phonological short-term memory				100			
Rapid automatic naming		80					
Tests: Attainments							
Reading accuracy – single word				102			
Reading comprehension (untimed)				94			
Reading speed (silent)				95			
Sight-word reading (timed)			85				
Non-word reading (timed)				105			
Spelling – single word		84					
Free writing: handwriting speed		71					
Copying speed		72					
Mathematical reasoning		83					
Further Tests							
Visual motor integration		74					

This layout is limited to standard scores only for the purposes of presenting a brief case study; assessors will wish to adapt their own score presentation style to include further test and technical detail (see Chapter 8).

Joanna presented a very different picture. Her case history revealed a host of difficulties with fine motor skills since infancy – using cutlery, dressing, cutting and sticking and so on. Seen in this developmental perspective, her awkward pencil grip and untidy handwriting suggest specific difficulties with motor coordination. This conclusion is supported by her weak performance on the non-verbal ability tests, copying tasks and tests for motor skills.

Joanna's verbal abilities, phonological awareness and word-level reading and reading comprehension were all comfortably within the average/high average range for her age. Her spelling was fully alphabetic (e.g. *booles* for *bullies*) but weaker than her reading. The 'careless' mistakes she often makes when writing (for example, *qwik* for *quick*) stemmed in part from not having established secure motor patterns for common words, as well as having a weaker recall of visual patterns of words.

An analysis of her handwriting showed that size of mid-zone letters, height of ascenders, and letters not sitting on the line were the chief problems. A programme to address these difficulties was suggested. It was agreed that the quantity of written work expected from her in class and for homework would be reduced and the use of writing frames was recommended. There were plans to develop her touch-typing skills and increase her use of the computer. Her writing speed would be monitored with a view to perhaps applying for additional time during her Key Stage 2 tests.

The implications of her slow processing speed and weak verbal memory were discussed, for example when trying to follow instructions and explanations or do mental arithmetic. Strategies to reduce these difficulties were recommended to Joanna and her teacher.

Taking all the evidence into account, the assessment revealed a profile characteristic of dyspraxia and referral was made to an Occupational Therapist to investigate this conclusion and to gain additional information on appropriate support.

Summary

Individual assessment was able to identify each child's good attainments, acknowledge and specify the difficulties and suggest ways of addressing them. The children themselves, their parents and teachers were provided with the information they needed to create constructive and relevant support programmes and adjustments.

12 The Secondary Phase

At secondary level, the nature and organisation of education bring new challenges for both pupils and assessors. Assessors need to adapt to a variety of contexts as well as support pupils through key transitions, into secondary school from primary and onward to the world beyond compulsory education. They will also be supporting pupils through perhaps some of the most challenging years of their development. Throughout this time, it becomes harder to capture a full picture of the pupil who is working in many different subject areas and with many different teachers.

The transition to secondary school

The transition to secondary school can be challenging for many pupils and those with an SpLD often find it particularly so. Pupils who managed to cope at primary school may find their specific difficulties emerge now, as they contend with many new demands, for example:

- more teachers, numerous classrooms in different locations and a complicated timetable needing different equipment on different days;
- more and new subjects, with an increasing amount of subject-specific vocabulary, as well as words which have different meanings in different settings (e.g. *scale, set, bug, file*);
- more reading and writing demands in most subjects, and more homework;
- more demands for rote learning (e.g. foreign vocabulary, formulae);
- new and higher-level demands of work and organisation.

Subject teachers at secondary level may not know how best to help pupils with poor literacy skills.[1] They are skilled in teaching their specialist subjects, but even teachers of English will not necessarily have been trained to teach the early stages of reading and writing. The assessor's knowledge will therefore be particularly helpful when making recommendations and providing guidance to support pupils in these areas.

Indicators of difficulties

While difficulties seen during the primary school years might persist into the secondary years, this may not be the case if there has been effective intervention. What may not be obvious is that literacy skills apparently mastered have not

---

[1] The Literacy and Dyslexia-SpLD Professional Development Framework can help teachers develop their knowledge in this area: http://framework.thedyslexia-spldtrust.org.uk

reached the stage of being automatic, so that reading and writing tasks are often more effortful for the pupil with a specific learning difficulty.

The areas of concern are likely to include the following:

Reading

- inaccurate reading (e.g. misreading examination questions); slow reading; losing the thread of longer texts; poor skimming and scanning skills, and trouble identifying the main idea.

Spelling and Writing

- use of restricted vocabulary that is easier to spell, masking the true level of understanding and expression;
- legibility and speed of handwriting; punctuation and presentation; difficulties in proof-reading own work;
- difficulties with transferring ideas on to paper. For example, analysing and writing in sufficient detail, expressing the salient points clearly, planning, organising and sequencing material, creating a coherent structure;
- ineffective note-taking skills from books or in lessons (difficulty listening and writing at the same time).

Learning

- difficulties in acquiring subject-specific vocabulary; understanding, reading and spelling technical words;
- difficulties in studying a foreign language.

Unusual contrasts

- a disparity between oral contributions in class and written work;
- a disparity between the quality of classwork, homework or coursework produced without a time limit and work written under timed conditions, such as examinations; consistent inability to finish examination papers in time;
- tiring more easily than peers; more prone to examination stress.

Organisation and Memory

- personal organisation: having the right equipment and materials in the right place, at the right time; time-keeping and meeting deadlines.

Emotional

- low levels of confidence or fragile self-esteem, possibly leading to bullying, or behaviour problems and truancy.

Purposes of assessment

The key purpose will be to support the pupil in his learning, through the recommendations and support plan arising from the assessment. It might also be to support pupils over 16 going on to Further or Higher Education; those going to University will need a report which meets SASC guidelines.

Assessments might also be needed to consider examination access arrangements. Given the significance of externally marked examinations, parents, pupils and teachers often request this kind of assessment. For many general and vocational qualifications, the Joint Council for Qualifications (JCQ) oversees the regulations relevant to when arrangements such as extra time, or a reader, might be allowed.[2] Some examination boards – for example, the International Baccalaureate and a number of vocational courses – have their own regulations. Keeping up to date with regulations will be needed. It is helpful if the assessor also makes recommendations to support the ongoing work of the pupil and not only his performance in examinations.

Any independent practitioners carrying out examination access assessments should be aware that they must be approved by the Head of Centre and collaborate closely with Centre staff. It is also considered good practice for the assessor to hold a current Assessment Practising Certificate.

Assessment at secondary level

Diagnostic assessments will follow core practice guidelines as discussed in Chapter 5, but here we reflect on a few additional points of note for the secondary assessor.

Firstly, when choosing tests for secondary-aged students, it is particularly important to ensure that the test age-ranges are appropriate: some well-known tests have their 'ceiling' at around 13 years of age. Also, the materials must be relevant for those 11 years and older; care will be needed to avoid denting what might be a fragile self-esteem.

The precise choice of tests will be determined by the purpose of the assessment. However, when testing at secondary level, it is worth noting that pupils who have fallen behind will often demonstrate unexpected difficulties for this age range, such as in basic phonics, common sequences, times tables and so on. A good principle is 'never assume anything' and be ready with additional material in order to explore these areas more fully. Informal review of difficulties with certain subjects or study skills might also be needed to plan an effective support programme.

Gathering background information

Collecting background information about the pupil prior to the assessment is essential. At secondary level, where the pupil has a number of teachers and his parents are less likely to come into school, perhaps the easiest way of gathering this information is through the use of questionnaires or checklists, one designed for home and another for school.

---

[2] For up-to-date information on current regulations, see www.jcq.org.uk. Guidance on application of the regulations can be found in the Patoss/JCQ publication *Dyslexia: Assessing the Need for Access Arrangements during Examinations, A Practical Guide*, 4th edition, edited by A. Jones.

Responses to questions from home should enable the assessor to identify at-risk factors associated with a specific learning difficulty, such as family history and late speech development, and to highlight any indicators of dyslexia, such as delay in learning to read.

Subject teachers can provide invaluable information about how well an individual copes in the classroom, and reviewing this information might reveal not only recurring strengths and weaknesses, but also inconsistencies between performances in different subjects. Their input might be gained by enlisting the help of the SENCO or the year tutor, depending on the school. A telephone call to key staff to discuss the pupil will greatly improve the quality of the information obtained and help to foster the cooperative approach needed with this dynamic process. Requests for information should always be measured and reasonable in light of teachers' other duties.

The pupil himself is also an important source of information at this stage. He is generally able to explain where his strengths and weaknesses lie, what he has found helpful or frustrating, as well as his current aims, ambitions and particular concerns.

Cognitive abilities

As well as individual testing of verbal and non-verbal ability, the pupil's language abilities can be considered during the course of the assessment conversation. His ability both to express himself clearly and respond appropriately should be noted, and observations might be compared with comments from his teachers about his contributions in class. There might be additional comment about his expressive language skills when communicating informally, for example with his friends.

If a receptive-expressive verbal ability test shows weaknesses, a separate receptive vocabulary test might be useful, especially for those pupils who appear to have word-finding difficulties, or those who are perhaps more reticent, or where teachers raise concerns about any unwillingness to join in class discussion. A good score can be encouraging as it will indicate academic potential and augur well for the pupil's ability to benefit from the spoken language of the classroom. A weak score may indicate that the pupil will struggle to access the learning and teaching as expected, or it may reflect a lack of reading experience, as we know that reading feeds increasingly into vocabulary acquisition as pupils grow up.

Group testing of underlying ability is common in schools, but these tests are designed as brief measures to be used in a screening process and as such they may produce unreliable or misleading results for the student with an SpLD. The style of the response sheet, often in a grid format, or the pupil's weaknesses in processing speed, working memory, literacy skills, attention or concentration, might affect the outcome. Crucially, group testing removes the valuable opportunity to look at strategies used by the student when tackling the tasks.

Memory, phonological and processing abilities will be assessed as for all assessments.

Attainments

Reading

As usual, a range of standardised reading tasks will be administered. A comprehensive profile of the pupil's strategies in a variety of contexts will allow for more accurate and specific targets for support.

A good knowledge of reading tests for this age group is very helpful when considering which is best to use for a particular pupil. Some tests might be less intimidating because of the way they are administered; others incorporate a range of different sub-skills of reading. Where comprehension tests require reading aloud, this might disadvantage those whose efforts to decode leave little capacity or energy for understanding.

In most cases at this level, pupils will have developed basic segmentation and blending skills, although perhaps without ease or fluency. It is often the lack of automaticity which holds the key to understanding why literacy skills have not developed as expected and therefore timed tests, both at the single-word and text level, can give important information.

Silent reading tests play an important part in testing at secondary level because fluency becomes a significant issue as the amount of reading increases, especially during examination courses. Those reading tests that are timed are particularly relevant for gauging the need for additional time allowances during examinations, since they reflect the examination situation quite well.

Additional testing often provides valuable insights as to how the pupil can be helped, such as informal checking on the pupil's reading of words needed in specific subjects, or comparison between a listening comprehension and a silent reading comprehension to uncover whether difficulties with comprehension are language based, or due to a difficulty with reading accuracy. If an informal listening comprehension is chosen, age-appropriate text can be read aloud and the pupil asked questions to test both literal and inferential understanding – i.e. not only his ability to recall factual information (*who, what, where, when*, etc), but also his ability to *infer* from the text.

Spelling

Some spelling tests provide more detailed information than others, useful diagnostically. Others follow the normal development of spelling and range from high- to low-frequency words, enabling the assessor to describe the individual spelling profile and pinpoint a starting point for teaching. Single-word spelling can also be checked informally using lists from Key Stages and subject-specific vocabulary lists.

When analysing spelling, much greater information than simply the score is needed. Pupils with identical spelling scores may be at different stages of development. Spelling errors can be 'good' errors (i.e. phonetically acceptable, thus readable) or completely bizarre, with little mapping of sound-symbol correspondences. In each case the marks are the same, but the implications for recommendations are very different.

Writing

For pupils with an SpLD, it is often in the area of writing, both in quality and quantity, where difficulties are most persistent. Replicating the writing demands of the classroom in an assessment situation is challenging, therefore it is particularly helpful to gather supplementary evidence of the pupil's written work, completed independently in different subjects. A comparison of writing under timed and untimed conditions is also useful.

Writing samples should be evaluated qualitatively by considering the various components and the balance between them. For example, a familiar pattern in dyslexia is that the quality of language and ideas might be good, while spelling, technical accuracy and organisation of ideas are weak.

Word level: spelling accuracy in composition (and percentage of words misspelt; compare to single-word spelling); legibility (and percentage of words unreadable); level and range of vocabulary used.

Sentence level: sentence structure; grammar; punctuation.

Text level: content; organisation of information; paragraphing skills; use of ideas; level of creativity; analysis of the speed of writing is of particular importance, given how much writing is expected during this phase of education; timed copying tasks will be useful to separate out the speed, control and fluency of the handwriting from other components of expressive writing.

Mathematics

As shown in the case study of Abdul at the end of this chapter, a combination of formal and informal tests will explore what the difficulties are and importantly where and why the skills are breaking down.

It might be discovered that the real problem is not particularly with maths skills, but with weak literacy and/or language skills which would impact on:

- understanding and interpreting questions;
- matching vocabulary to concepts, formulae and operations;
- documenting the thinking process when writing up investigations.

Recommendations will identify how individuals might manage the demands they would expect to meet across the curriculum, as well as particular teaching needs.

Observation and questioning

It is always important to observe and investigate the strategies used by the pupil. Once the pupil has completed a test, questions can be asked about how he arrived at the answers, without invalidating the results.

Observation during the assessment provides important diagnostic information by giving an insight into the amount of time and effort expended on tasks. A pupil may use a range of strategies to cope with literacy and numeracy tasks. He may, for example, sub-vocalise, perhaps because this strategy helps him to access the meaning of text, or because fast automatised reading is not yet mastered. He may track text with a pen or finger to keep his place when reading. He might have to re-read the passage in order to answer comprehension questions, or not be able to answer in his own words, but only quote verbatim from the text. He might have found ingenious ways to add, or multiply numbers.

This observation is needed as pupils can gain identical scores, but have very different strategies and skills. For example, reading accuracy scores are based on the number of words read correctly, but the pupil who misreads small words such as *to, of, for* may derive more meaning from the text than the pupil who lacks the word-attack skills to cope with polysyllabic words containing more of the content. Miscue analysis is a useful technique for analysing the reading strategies which lead to errors (see page 173).

It would also be important to ascertain any strategies the pupil used in other tests. For example, memory is a complex skill to assess, as it is often affected by other factors such as attention, concentration and levels of anxiety. Questions will clarify if the pupil was drawing on memorising strategies other than those being tested, such as *visualising* letters or numbers in a test of *verbal* memory. If he expends a great deal of effort to succeed, could this be maintained in the busy secondary environment?

Such information can be used as supporting evidence when describing individual strengths and weaknesses. The assessor can also use this information to help formulate a teaching programme which utilises the strategies already used, or to recommend developing alternative ones.

Outcomes of assessment

Assessment will help to uncover the nature and cause of the pupil's problems, and in a good number of cases it will be possible to identify a diagnostic label. Knowing that there is a name for the difficulty is often a source of relief for the pupil and those working with him, but while it can be very helpful, it is not sufficient on its own to move the situation forwards.

The assessment findings must be used to explain his strengths and weaknesses. Encouraging the pupil to understand how he learns best is a powerful way of helping him to learn effectively and by doing so, improve his motivation and performance. This is the first step to enable him to work on difficulties with a realistic and positive self-image.

Some secondary school pupils are easily disaffected and working towards goals imposed by teachers is not necessarily the first priority! Therefore, engaging him in his own target-setting is important. It is particularly relevant when planning an intervention programme. Relating targets and goals to his interests is the essence of nurturing metacognitive awareness and independence.

Report format and recommendations

It is recommended that full diagnostic assessments follow the outline pro-forma set out by SASC. If a diagnostic conclusion is not needed, or time or resources do not allow, the assessor might produce a more brief report, including an explanation of the assessment tasks, an analysis and discussion of the pupil's performance, together with the recommendations and targets. The evidence provided by the scores can be included in an appendix. Diagnostic reports of whatever style will be a valuable way of communicating findings, so that the pupil can be supported in the varied settings within secondary school and teachers can respond effectively to specific difficulties and differences in the ways that pupils learn.

Commonly the main focus of support will be in the realms of study skills, firmly tied into curriculum work, but it should be borne in mind that some pupils will still need help at a much more basic level. Poor readers will continue to have difficulty accessing the curriculum, no matter how highly organised they are. Thus specialist teaching may need to prioritise underpinning literacy skills. However, this should, as far as possible, be relevant to the subjects the pupil is studying. Revisiting phonics programmes that have been worked on before is likely to alienate an adolescent.

Recommendations could include targets for:

Reading fluency and confidence: Paired reading schemes with older pupils supporting younger pupils; reading simplified versions of novels and plays; watching the film/video/play; working with the audio version and 'pair reading' with the book. Using the index, chapter summaries, skimming and scanning techniques; listening to audio books.

Study skills: Note-taking and memory skills; organisation of time, belongings and homework.

Preparing for examinations: Revision and learning techniques – consider when, where and how. Question analysis; practice of timed questions. Planning, timetabling; managing stress levels.

Taking the examination: Techniques for accurate reading, accurate interpretation of questions; taking time to plan the answer.

Spelling: Focus on what is needed: morphemes; subject-specific vocabulary; a few useful spelling rules – for suffixing, plurals, etc. Use *spelling* dictionaries; personal spelling memo books or cards; electronic dictionaries and spell-checkers.

Writing: Use mind maps, time-lines, mind-mapping software; writing frames for planning; word processing for redrafting/editing. Look at different types of essays; how to build sentences and paragraphs and plan projects. If handwriting is arduous, slow and illegible, where appropriate, recommend assistive software or word processing.

Memory: Find out how memory works; memory techniques; use different personal strategies for rote learning and revision – visualisation, posters, mind maps, auditory input and multisensory techniques.

Numeracy: Consider personal learning style; consolidate knowledge of maths language and number facts; use bypass strategies such as number squares and calculators. Apply memory techniques to remember formulae. Look for ways to improve recording, particularly in longer investigations. Explore and visualise the language of maths. Look for examples from a real context. Draw or sketch maths problems. Repeating worksheets and textbook exercises is unlikely to be successful.

Case study: Abdul

Abdul is twelve years old. He enjoys school, particularly sports and technology, but is having ongoing difficulty in mathematics and finds English 'boring'. His recent school cognitive ability scores were all within average bands, but he is in a low set for maths and has not received any support.

All developmental milestones were reached at an appropriate age and he is physically well coordinated. He is a normally happy and well-adjusted boy who wants to be an engineer.

Abdul (age 12 years)

	-3	-2	-1	0	+1	+2	+3
Standard Deviation	-3	-2	-1	0	+1	+2	+3
Standard Score	69-	70-84	85-89	90-110	111-115	116-130	131+
				Broad average range			
Tests: Cognitive Abilities							
Verbal ability			89				
Non-verbal ability					115		
Phonological awareness: segmentation		72					
Phonological awareness: blending		74					
Phonological short-term memory		75					
Rapid automatic naming				90			
Visual processing speed (written)				94			
Verbal working memory		70					
Visual memory				109			

Tests: Literacy Skills							
Reading accuracy – single word				98			
Sight-word reading (timed)				92			
Non-word reading (timed)		80					
Prose reading speed			88				
Reading comprehension (untimed)		73					
Mathematical Reasoning Test			86				
Spelling – single word			85				
Copying speed				107			
Free writing: handwriting speed			87				

This layout is limited to standard scores only for the purposes of presenting a brief case study; assessors will wish to adapt their own score presentation style to include further test and technical detail (see Chapter 8).

Abdul learns from this assessment that his particular difficulties with mathematics are not to do with numbers. In fact, he is good at calculation! Rather he has specific problems with verbal working memory and comprehension. In class it is the reading and interpretation of maths questions which are difficult for him. This explanation was meaningful to Abdul as he reported finding questions involving fractions difficult to understand; he did not know the meaning of *sixth, third*, etc. He could demonstrate the correct procedure for working out a lowest common multiple, but he did not know what it all meant. He also said he liked shapes but he could not remember their names.

His reluctance to read and his dislike of English was unsurprising given his weak comprehension of text. Miscue analysis showed he did not make good use of context cues when reading, so promoting use of 'top down' strategies was also recommended in the report.

He is reassured that his difficulty is a specific one. While his non-verbal ability and practical skills fall at the top of the high-average range, he has dyslexia with characteristic weaknesses in verbal working memory and phonological awareness, as well as a relative weakness in visual processing speed when compared to the broader ability levels he demonstrated in measures of non-verbal ability.

Understanding his own strengths will help him to utilise his good visual-spatial ability generally and in particular enable him to develop his skills in areas of the maths curriculum such as shape and space and graph work.

Multisensory teaching methods will show him how to use all his senses to work more effectively. In particular, his teacher is going to explain maths words and concepts by linking real-life examples to visual (diagrams), verbal and symbolic representations, making sure that Abdul himself does the drawing and writing.

Case study: Susie

Susie is fifteen years old. She has always struggled with reading and spelling and there is a family history of spelling difficulties. There were no problems with her early development, although her medical history shows that she suffers from migraines and is asthmatic. Although shy, she is popular in school and gets on well with peers and adults. Normally well-adjusted, she is becoming anxious and her confidence is reported to be fragile.

She lacks fluency and speed when reading; she uses her fingers to track her place and she does not comprehend easily. She tends to spell phonetically, but this strategy does not always work with longer words. She frequently finds it hard to understand what is being asked of her.

Susie *(age 15 years)*

	−3	−2	−1	0	+1	+2	+3
Standard Deviation	−3	−2	−1	0	+1	+2	+3
Standard Score	69−	70–84	85–89	90–110	111–115	116–130	131+
				Broad average range			
Tests: Cognitive Abilities							
Verbal ability				105			
Non-verbal ability				95			
Phonological awareness: segmentation	66						
Phonological awareness: blending		72					
Phonological Short-term Memory		78					
Rapid Automatic Naming		70					
Visual Processing Speed (written)		75					
Verbal Working Memory		78					
Visual Memory			88				
Tests: Literacy Skills							
Reading accuracy – single word				102			
Sight-word reading (timed)		84					
Non-word reading (timed)	68						
Reading speed				92			
Reading comprehension (untimed)			87				
Spelling – single word		76					
Copying speed				95			
Free writing speed: handwriting			88				

This layout is limited to standard scores only for the purposes of presenting a brief case study; assessors will wish to adapt their own score presentation style to include further test and technical detail (see Chapter 8).

Susie learns from her assessment that she has a sound level of reasoning ability. Her spelling is generally logical but her visual recall of letter patterns is insecure. Her handwriting is excellent and her written work is legible and well presented. As she prefers to handwrite her examinations and her spellings are decipherable, she chooses not to use a scribe. Her reading accuracy at word level is sound for her age, but she has difficulty processing information at speed, so her rate of reading is slow. Her difficulties are typical of dyslexia since the primary problem is the application of her phonic knowledge. Being taught about syllable division will be important and enable her to tackle longer words when writing. Linked to this will be the development of skills in using a spell checker effectively.

Susie's school will apply for extra time in examinations to compensate for her below-average reading and processing speeds. With her difficulties acknowledged and practical plans for addressing them in place, her self-esteem and confidence are boosted.

Summary

- Particular difficulties arise at the secondary stage because of the more fragmented nature of the curriculum and its increasing demands on higher-level literacy skills.
- Some students continue to experience difficulties at a basic level which subject teachers are not really trained to deal with.
- Others find that the increasing demands of the curriculum present challenges to their study and organisation skills, as well as their ability to read and write fluently.
- Examinations become a major concern.
- Self-esteem is often fragile.
- Appropriate assessment resources cover many of the same areas as at the primary stage – but they must be age-appropriate and relate to the skills needed at this stage.
- The student himself is a primary source of information at this level. He must be an active partner in both the assessment and in setting targets.
- The aim is for him, as well as his teachers and parents, to have a clearer picture of his strengths, difficulties and best ways of working.

13 Further Education

Professionals working in Further Education (FE) face an entirely different set of demands, constraints and possibilities to those working elsewhere in education. It is here where assessors are likely to meet the greatest diversity of students and meeting individual needs in a timely fashion is a challenge indeed.

The FE environment – particular considerations

The sheer variety in FE is enormous. Students fresh from school are mixed with older students returning to study. From health and beauty students, to gas engineers, to animal care students, to art students, to those re-taking GCSEs, or following adult literacy programs, or working towards Foundation degrees, the range of topics studied, the nature of the courses and the stories of the students following them are endlessly varied. Those working in this wonderfully diverse world need to know the territory. Many features of the terrain will seem unfamiliar to those more used to other sectors of education.

To begin with, the terminology is different. In FE, terms such as students with *Learning Difficulties and Disabilities* (LDD), or students with *additional support needs*, replace the *Special Educational Needs* phrase used in schools. LDD is an umbrella term that includes SpLDs. Commonly there is a 'Learning Support Department' to coordinate services rather than the 'Disability Service' found in universities.

Funding arrangements are also different. Additional learning support funding comes to colleges, not to individuals, through complex mechanisms which require colleges to provide detailed evidence of need across their cohort. This drives the requirement for careful initial screening of all students and comprehensive support records. As the focus is on evidence of need, students do not have to be formally diagnosed with an SpLD to qualify for support. (However, funding for those following HE courses is available through the Disabled Students' Allowance.)

Many students arrive without a documented history of their difficulties and there is less time to observe and investigate their needs in FE than in school, especially for part-time students. Therefore, the sooner the identification of need takes place, the better. The ideal would be for all students to be screened in the first week of their college courses.

Screening in FE

Screening can involve a paper-based assessment of literacy and numeracy skills, but in many colleges such tests have been replaced with computerised packages that offer a baseline assessment of these skills. Many students are attracted to FE because they have not fared too well in academic subjects at school and are hoping for a fresh start. Spelling and grammar might not be their strong points. Their talents might be more likely to include an ability to detect a badly-tuned engine or to spot an ideal composition for a photograph. Their hopes will quickly be dashed if they are subjected to an insensitive assessment of their literacy and numeracy skills within the first few days of college. Therefore, vulnerable groups might find a paper-based screening process less threatening, and their tutors might find the information it generates more useful. This could include tasks in note-taking, reading, spelling and summarising a passage of text, which use course-related materials and vocabulary, as well as an opportunity for students to consider independently their learning strengths and styles. Tutors with experience of students with SpLDs will be able to spot characteristic traits in the material produced. Specialist assessors are well placed to advise course tutors who wish to develop this kind of more detailed screening. (See alternative screening notes in Part 4.)

There are also computerised screening programmes that purport to identify those students who are likely to have dyslexia. The advantage of such tests is that they are relatively quick to administer and analysis is done automatically. However, we are not necessarily looking for a diagnostic label in the FE setting; we are seeking to identify individual needs. In this respect, while these computerised packages might provide a starting point, they might not give a sufficiently detailed picture of the student to plan effective support.

As part of the screening process, it is always worth asking students to note if they have had examination access arrangements or diagnostic assessments in the past – even if they were asked at application stage. The student might now be ready to say he had a reader and extra time and his teacher always said she thought he might have dyslexia.

General screening processes, or specially designed screening tests for SpLDs, are far from 100% reliable in identifying students with possible SpLD. Therefore, mainstream staff can be asked to refer individual students who have been missed. A checklist might help staff to identify such students more easily. This referral could provide both helpful diagnostic information and evidence of the student's normal way of working for any examination access arrangements.

The following might form a useful basis of a checklist – staff could answer yes/no, but also be offered the opportunity to comment on each point if they wished.

Referral checklist for academic FE staff

Please reflect on typical standards for your group, and consider the following for the student.

Is he or she:
- well motivated, yet submitting work late or lacking the depth you expect?
- producing written work of a much weaker standard than spoken contributions?
- making bizarre spelling mistakes?
- making uncharacteristic spelling mistakes in word-processed work?
- writing with poor structure – for example with missing words or incorrect tenses – in contrast to use when speaking?
- unwilling to read aloud in class?
- having difficulty taking notes?
- unable to concentrate even when interested and ready to learn?
- having difficulty managing and organising time or learning materials to an unusual degree?
- experiencing greater difficulty with numeracy than expected, given their other abilities?
- gaining much weaker results in timed test conditions than in coursework submissions?
- consistently in need of extra time for reading and writing in class tasks and tests?
- producing writing very slowly or illegibly?
- using a word processor consistently in class?
- regularly in need of reading support?
- attending additional learning support?
- regularly using help from in-class learning support assistants?
- regularly in need of a prompt to re-focus attention on the task in hand?

Individual assessment in FE

Although support systems in FE do not demand it, some individuals might choose the option of a further, in-depth diagnostic assessment. At the outset the student should be made aware of how results will be used. For example, will results go to work placement supervisors? Or parents? Or tutors? As adults, all students in FE must be consulted on how their private data is to be shared and a written consent is recommended.

As the range of ability and attainment in FE is so great, assessors will need a wide selection of formal and informal tests to ensure they have to hand an appropriate task to suit the individual – to supplement, or sometimes replace, tests in the standard battery. (Those students going on to HE will need assessments which meet standards appropriate for university.) Therefore, what follows is a discussion of the additional materials an FE assessor might want to have available. Assessors will also find a wealth of informal and useful assessment resources at: www.excellencegateway.org.uk

Background information

In the case of most FE students, background information will be gathered by discussion. Some will not have the confidence to complete a questionnaire independently. Questions along the lines of *'Many people find it difficult to organise their thoughts on paper – would you say that applied to you?'* are more conducive to an honest discussion than *'Do you have a problem organising your ideas?'* It is such a subtle distinction, but it can make all the difference in the world to a nervous student who may be grateful to know that he is not on his own.

Self-reporting of background information comes to the fore at this stage – parents are less likely to be involved and often tutors are only just getting to know students. Written permission must be gained before background information is sought from external sources such as previous schools. Where student comments are relied on, assessors should use careful questioning and adopt a somewhat cautious approach in interpreting this data – although there is certainly no need to disregard it. For example, entirely innocently, students might state that they have been previously diagnosed with dyslexia, although questioning reveals that this is based only on an informal comment from a teacher.

In evaluating students' descriptions of their current difficulties, the FE assessor, as in every sector, will take into account the typical challenges faced by all students at their level of study. It is unusual or unexpected patterns which are of interest in a diagnostic assessment.

Cognitive abilities

Underlying and specific cognitive abilities will be tested in line with standard practice. However, some further reflection on this cohort's needs is warranted.

There are students right across the ability range enrolled in FE. Those with high or average underlying abilities will usually find cognitive testing interesting and the results supportive. Through their careful test delivery, assessors must ensure that those with lower abilities – or those whose abilities are outside the domains included in traditional tests – have an equally positive experience, even if the results are more challenging to report.

In regard to cognitive processing, useful informal measures of phonological awareness abilities are included in materials designed to support the adult literacy curriculum for FE and might be needed to supplement standardised tests. These are most likely to be useful where a specialist teacher will subsequently be providing intensive support, but might also be valuable in exploring and evidencing the nature of the student's difficulty.

Attainments

It is not unusual to meet students who, for one reason or another, have extremely limited literacy skills. Be prepared for this and spare them the humiliation of being asked to do something beyond their capabilities.

For instance, to ask students with very weak skills to produce timed writing on a given topic will be a complete non-starter – a far better approach would be to ask what things they can write. This might be a job-related writing task or a greeting on a Christmas card. In order to plan steps forward, the comfortable follow-up from this is to ask what they would like to be able to write. For other students, assessors might reflect on the type of writing task needed for the course and devise an informal task based on that information. A copying or dictation task might be useful to inspect working memory or motor coordination difficulties in more detail.

Similarly, for those with very limited reading skills, tests which are designed to cover the whole FE/HE cohort may prove too difficult. Students might reach the stopping point for the test long before sufficient useful data has been gained about reading strategies, and tests designed for lower reading abilities, often designed for children, are inappropriate because of content themes. The way forward is to use a selection of formal and informal test materials. A view of the student's reading level and reading interests must be taken, using screening results, background information, course level and results of a formal single-word reading test, and then on-the-hoof decisions taken about where to go next.

Can this student manage a formal reading comprehension test of continuous text? Would a sentence-level task be more appropriate? Is a standard score needed for purposes such as examination access arrangements? Would an informal piece of reading drawn from course material be useful in addition? Are different informal materials needed for older students in contrast to teenage students? Would a check of single-word reading of course-related words be useful? Often the answer to all of these questions is 'yes'.

Thus, the FE assessor could work towards having available a collection of material suitable to match the age, stage, interests, courses and reading level of their students. Once they are devised, these materials can be used again and again to give valuable qualitative data which cannot be conveyed by a simple standard score.

It might also be necessary to check knowledge of sound-symbol correspondence and the alphabet; surprising numbers of students over 16 with an SpLD have not mastered these skills. Handled with care to avoid the implication of a childhood task, this adds to the diagnostic picture and informs teaching. Assessors can explain this is a normal part of testing for all – most students are happy to oblige.

Numeracy

Many students in FE find, often to their horror, that they must again tackle mathematics. A diagnostic assessment is therefore quite likely to include numeracy. Weaknesses in everyday numeracy skills are known to have an even greater negative impact on later success in adult life than weak literacy skills, so this area must not be lightly set aside. Screening results will provide a measure of achievement, but little in the way of strategies, stumbling blocks, methods of working or areas of relative strength. FE can often provide wonderful opportunities to learn in a new way and assessors can highlight a specific need for different methods and approaches to mathematics teaching.

Feedback and report format

As in every sector, there is a need to allow time at the end of the assessment for a discussion of all that has taken place. Ideally, the student should also be invited to a follow-up session, once the report has been prepared, so that they have a chance to read and discuss it before it is passed to other parties. If face-to-face feedback is not possible, a compromise might be to include with the report a covering letter addressed to the student, with a straightforward overview of the findings using language which is accessible to the individual.

Given the pressures of limited resources, it might be wise to consider whether or not a full diagnostic assessment report is always needed. Those students over 16 who are considering Higher Education or further professional or vocational training will need a report which meets SASC guidelines (www.sasc.org.uk), and many other students, and their parents and teachers, will find a full report immensely useful. However, for others, such a lengthy and detailed document would be beyond their current reading skills and is not needed to secure support. In these cases assessors might devise a summary report, although the assessment will have been just as thorough. For example, this shortened report could adopt the same format, but be written in a less formal style with the focus firmly on discussion of strengths and weaknesses found, plus the conclusion. A visual display of scores would be useful to show the profile contrasts. Use could be made throughout of bullet points rather than extended prose. Most important would be detailed recommendations. Such a document would still need to include sufficient data to substantiate the conclusion and this might be given in a technical appendix with a table of scores.

Recommendations and teaching/support programmes

As ever, recommendations in FE must closely match the assessment findings and the individual's need, current context and future plans. However, the following issues should also be considered.

Firstly, there is the issue of whether an individual teaching programme is required. For some students, the screening process will encourage them to request an in-depth assessment and they will seek active teaching and support to address their difficulties.

There will be other students who request an in-depth assessment more to satisfy an inner curiosity as to why it was they fared so badly at school, despite a sneaking suspicion that they were at least as bright as their higher-achieving peers. The members of this group are just seeking an explanation and an opportunity to discuss all that has been suppressed over the years. They will not necessarily need teaching recommendations as well.

For those who do need individual teaching or support programmes, the emphasis is more likely to be weighted towards subject vocabulary, study skills, reading comprehension, writing planning and examination preparation, rather than structured phonics programmes and word-level work. A balance has to be struck between the student's understandable concern to complete current work with teaching him useful underlying skills and strategies. All targets will be negotiated with the student and he will be involved in their evaluation. As regards methods and resources, underlying multisensory principles still apply and adults are often very willing to adopt them as long as the rationale is fully explained.

In providing support to FE students, there is the added complication of fitting in with commitments outside college, course schedules and weeks out of college on work experience. The positive side of the variation is that there are opportunities for one-to-one work without the issue of withdrawal from mainstream classes that can cause difficulties in school; offering flexible teaching times which suit the student's circumstances will increase motivation and so the possibilities for success.

Summary

- The population of a typical FE college is one of considerable diversity in terms of the range of age, ability and educational experience of its students.
- Funding for Additional Learning Support goes to the college rather than the student. Funding is available only where there is clear evidence of need. The need does not require the formal label of a specific learning difficulty.
- This need has to be identified at the earliest opportunity. Comprehensive screening of all new students is just as important as in-depth diagnostic assessment of a much smaller number.
- Diagnostic assessment in FE follows standard practice, but a range of additional informal materials relating to the individual's course and age is useful for full understanding of their strengths and weaknesses.
- Any programmes resulting from these in-depth assessments must be negotiated with the student and delivered in age-appropriate ways.

Case study: **Chloe** (aged 24)

Standard Deviation		-3	-2	-1	0	+1	+2	+3
Standard Score		69–	70–84	85–89	90–110	111–115	116–130	131+
					Broad average range			
Tests: Cognitive Abilities								
Verbal ability					104			
Non-verbal ability					107			
Phonological awareness			73					
Phonological short-term memory				85				
Rapid automatic naming			74					
Visual processing speed (written)			84					
Verbal working memory			76					
Visual memory					95			
Tests: Literacy Skills								
Reading accuracy – single word					90			
Reading comprehension (untimed)				85				
Sight-word reading (timed)			80					
Non-word reading (timed)			72					
Spelling – single word			79					
Non-standardised tests								
Reading speed: aloud		101 words per minute – below expectation						
Reading speed: silent		110 words per minute – below expectation						
Free writing speed: handwriting		15 words per minute – below expectation						
Free writing speed: word processing		16 words per minute – below expectation						

This layout is limited to standard scores only for the purposes of presenting a brief case study; assessors will wish to adapt their own score presentation style to include further test and technical detail (see Chapter 8).

Pre-assessment information: Chloe referred herself for assessment. She reported confidence in expressing her ideas in class, but does not feel she is doing herself justice on paper in her Level 3 studies. Chloe said reading was 'very tiring' and that she often read late into the night to keep up. She felt her lecture notes were sparse and she felt embarrassed about her spelling errors and so preferred to use a word processor to write.

Assessment observations: When reading continuous text, Chloe made minor but frequent accuracy errors and she softly sub-vocalised when reading. Her writing was legible and well-structured, but exposed errors in spelling common words and she used a more limited vocabulary than expected – she reported choosing only words she could spell. Chloe repeatedly rephrased sentences when writing and said that quite often she could not think of the word she wanted to use, so chose another.

Commentary: The assessment showed Chloe had reliable underlying abilities and her spoken language skills were good. Wide language experience, with some support from a good visual memory, has enabled her to build her sight-word vocabulary. She relied almost entirely on visual approaches to read words and also checked her spelling by reviewing the overall 'look' of a word, although this was not always reliable. Weaknesses in phonological awareness and phonological processing speed mean that spelling and reading unfamiliar words is difficult and all the measures of her reading speeds are slow. Her working memory skills are weak and are a factor in the effort and time she must devote to reading comprehension, her difficulties in taking notes, and weaknesses in writing composition. Her writing speed is slow and the extent of vocabulary used is at odds with her spoken language abilities.

Outcome: The assessor concluded that Chloe has dyslexia. Did the assessment help her? Yes. Chloe now has more confidence in her abilities and a better understanding of her difficulties. Her assessor was able to discuss strategies with Chloe for helping with difficulties such as the development of her own 'shorthand' for taking notes; a specialist teacher will consider study-reading strategies to cut down on Chloe's study hours and techniques to support course-related spelling; she is going to try out assistive technology to help her with some reading and writing tasks. Visual approaches to revision have been suggested and examination arrangements recommended.

14 Higher Education

Within the Higher Education (HE) sector generally, there is wide awareness of dyslexia and specific learning difficulties and the impact that these conditions might have on individual performance. It is common for universities to have teams of support staff working within the disability services, providing expert guidance and practical support for those with specific learning difficulties as they move through their degree courses.

However, in HE, as in other sectors, there are particular considerations for specialist assessors and we turn to these now.

Working within the HE sector

Specialist teachers assessing students for HE must hold a current Assessment Practising Certificate (APC), particularly if there is a possibility that an application for DSA might follow, and update it every three years by undertaking Continuing Professional Development and taking part in a review of their professional practice. Practitioner psychologists assessing students in HE must be registered with the Health and Care Professions Council (HCPC). All assessors must state their APC/Registration number in the diagnostic report.

Disabled Students' Allowance

UK students studying full or part time on a recognised course in England can apply for the Disabled Students' Allowance (DSA). This is a grant which provides students who have a specific learning difficulty, or any other disability, with the support they need to study on their course. There is much information available about the DSA and the process of application on Government web pages and often on University websites. There are separate but similar schemes for those studying in Wales, Scotland, Northern Ireland and the Open University, and for example for those studying on NHS bursaries.

Students applying for the DSA, or equivalent, will need a post-16 diagnostic report, which establishes the current impact of their specific difficulties on the skills needed for HE. They are encouraged to apply as early as possible, even before they secure their university places, in order that the appropriate support is in place from the start of their degree course. This means that all assessors working within the post-16 age group will need to follow SASC guidelines, so that their reports can be used for this purpose.

Test selection and report format

Tests should be drawn from the SASC approved list, although assessors may use additional resources if they wish, and the report should follow the published pro-forma (see www.patoss-dyslexia.org and www.sasc.org.uk).

Although schools and colleges have commendably tried to move away from labelling students, at university level, if students are to receive funding to support their disability needs, a clear diagnostic label is required. In cases of complex overlapping profiles, the assessor will be able to identify the dominant pattern, and where other characteristics co-exist, describe the presenting difficulties and the impact on learning and then make the appropriate educational recommendations. If there is no dominant pattern, a label of 'Specific Learning Difficulties' might be particularly useful, and this is acceptable to UK funding bodies.

However, it is certainly the case that not all students who come forward for assessment experience a *specific* difficulty and other factors should be considered. The world of HE is an increasingly varied one, and HE students are a widely heterogeneous group, in terms of age, educational background and academic qualifications. This means that some students embark on degree courses having received little in the way of formal training for essay writing, or coping with academic text, such that lack of study skills teaching is a factor, rather than an SpLD. Fortunately, in many universities, there is increasing general study support offered for those who need it, yet who fall outside formal disability provision.

More problematic is where assessment reveals an even, below-average test profile and the presence of general difficulties in learning. In such cases, sensitive advice needs to be given, if possible in liaison with the institution's support officers and combined with effective careers guidance.

Reasons for referral and indicators of difficulty at HE

Many students' difficulties are revealed for the first time at university. The increased level of study demands, including higher-order language use, as well as the need for greater independence in learning and in the organisation of study, can uncover problems which have gone unnoticed in the more structured school environment, or have been masked by enormous effort on the student's part.

In many courses there will be work placements, and the pressure and pace of new environments can highlight difficulties which were previously managed and not so apparent in academic study. Assessors need therefore to be alert to the variety of demands from different courses and be ready to make appropriate recommendations.

While the specific manifestations of difficulty will be as varied as the demands of the courses themselves, students' concerns are likely to be in the following areas:

Reading: speed and comprehension. Despite the fact that many students read for pleasure, having perfected a skim reading and prediction strategy, a recurring theme is the time it takes them to read and comprehend academic text, because they have been unable to develop additional reading strategies for different types of text. There may also be visual disturbance when reading, or concerns about misreading words, particularly under time pressure, as well as a fear of reading aloud in tutorials and seminars.

Writing skills: organising language and structuring ideas in written work. Even if sentence structure and paragraphing skills are sound, students may still be overwhelmed by the sheer volume and complexity of thoughts to be organised. Such students often turn in excellent course work, but this is the product of many drafts and the individual is therefore at a disadvantage in examinations, where extensive amendments are not an option.

Spelling: spelling skills often fragment under pressure. In examinations, anxiety about spelling may lead students to restructure their sentences in order to avoid problem words, or to use less appropriate ones, which disrupts writing fluency considerably.

Spoken language: students having problems with producing written work may also experience difficulty with spoken language. As a result, they contribute as little as possible in seminars, and dread verbal presentations.

Memory and organisation: students may struggle to remember names, numbers and to master unfamiliar academic/technical terms. Such problems also frequently compromise the ability to follow lectures and take effective notes. Mental calculation is slow and effortful and they have problems dealing with strictly sequenced material, such as an alphabetical index in libraries.

Students are often living away from home for the first time and they have to manage their lives in a more independent way. Weaknesses in organisation frequently show up in difficulties with time management, missing appointments/deadlines, managing and prioritising the very varied and multi-layered demands of some courses, as well as balancing study and home life.

Attention and concentration: students may find it difficult to maintain attention and focus on tasks such as reading, making notes, or sitting through a lecture and find themselves constantly distracted. As a result of the struggle to concentrate, they defer the tasks they find challenging and so fall behind. Procrastination and a feeling they cannot make decisions may also be problematic.

Other areas: a student may have been referred because of suspected dyslexia, but there might be additional difficulties and the assessor should also be alert to the possibility of other SpLDs and, as always, other reasons for difficulties beyond SpLD.

Screening

A 'screening' assessment is an initial form of assessment designed to give an indication as to whether the student has an SpLD. Typically, in universities, there are support staff who are able to carry out this initial screening and advise on the next steps.

Screening assessments can be organised in different ways, but a common method is to take the student through a face-to-face interview; a checklist might also be used, or the student will take a computerised screening test. In cases where the assessor works in close liaison with the HE institution, with the student's permission, the screening information may be made available, which is helpful. (See alternative screening method notes in Part 4.)

The assessment

Gathering background information

As we have stressed earlier, it is important to take a comprehensive background history. This may be gathered partly via a questionnaire completed before the assessment.

Assessors might like to gather information using the headings and questions in Figure 14.1 as a checklist.

Family history	Are any other family members affected by difficulties with written and/or spoken language?
General health	Vision and hearing – have these been checked? Eliminate the obvious. Is general health good, or is there anything which might have a bearing on the student's current difficulties? Have there been any recent changes or deterioration in health? Are there any other issues that are not documented but which could have an effect on the student's ability to study?
Speech and language	Check whether the student received speech therapy, and whether he recalls any problems with spoken language in the early years. Is he prone to word-finding difficulties, mispronunciations or word confusions now? Note the quality of oral explanations.
Linguistic history	If English is spoken as a second or additional language, the student's language history should be detailed and his current levels of competence in spoken and written English explored. Were there any difficulties with the original language noted?
Motor development	Was the student considered clumsy as a child? Did handwriting skills develop slowly? Did he receive any occupational therapy assessments? How is his fine and gross motor coordination now? Persistent motor coordination problems can indicate the presence of DCD (dyspraxia).
Educational history	Were literacy skills slow to develop? Was additional support received at any stage? Were there any previous educational assessments, or any previous examination access arrangements? Check earlier formal examination results, for example, GCSE and A-level results, as appropriate.
School experience	Were difficulties handled sensitively and was he well supported, or not? Did he feel able to access all areas of the curriculum? Were there frequent changes of school? Did the student have prolonged periods of absence or truanting?
Current difficulties	Explore current difficulties fully, including questions about tutor feedback (see 'Reasons for Referral and Indicators of Difficulties', above).

Figure 14.1

An opportunity to reflect before the assessment can be particularly helpful when, as in the case of some adult students, there is no history of learning experience or case history to provide guidance. However, some students may not know the details of their early development, or if, for example they had problems with speech and language development, or how easily they acquired reading and spelling skills.

Even when quite detailed information has been gathered in advance, the assessor will still need to allow time to explore the information presented and to probe any areas which need clarification. Such discussion gives insight into the student's main concerns, the motivation for the assessment and an opportunity to build rapport. This will be particularly important where the background information seems sketchy, or where the presenting problems seem to overlap with other specific learning difficulties.

Observation

At this level, the student might have developed effective compensatory strategies, and certain difficulties can be hard to detect. Careful observation during testing is, therefore, crucial, in order to produce an accurate assessment. There is, for example, a world of difference between two students who score 105 on a standardised spelling test, one with apparent ease, the other by thinking long and hard about each word, with multiple attempts. In the same way, circumlocutions and hesitations do not show up in final scores, yet will undoubtedly increase the difficulties with writing. Are there indicators of visual perceptual difficulties when reading, such as omission or repetition of lines, or does the student track lines of text with a pen or finger? Are working memory measures and/or phonological measures accompanied by a huge amount of effort, and possibly hand movement, which suggests the processing involved is a strain? It may be appropriate to use test behaviour as evidence of a difficulty when standardised scores belie the effort the student puts into tasks.

Issues for HE assessors in conducting assessments

There are assessors, both specialist teachers and practitioner psychologists, who carry out large numbers of assessments at HE level. When we are immersed in the world of dyslexia and provide diagnostic labels so frequently, it is too easy to forget the emotional impact that a diagnosis of a 'disability' can have on the student, and become desensitised to what it means to be labelled for the first time. We must remember that the purpose of diagnostic assessment at this level is not solely to produce a document making recommendations for examination adjustments and funding.

Thus, adequate time must be allowed for the assessment and it should be conducted in a patient and sensitive manner. Adult students – especially those being assessed for the first time – are likely to have questions which need to be answered and fears which need to be allayed before, during and after the assessment. While it can often be a relief for students to know that there is a recognised cause for their difficulties, some will have misgivings about labels. The assessor can help by explaining the outcome in terms of differences in learning style, by highlighting the student's strengths and discussing how these can be exploited in the learning process.

The assessor should be aware of the process for the student which follows the diagnostic assessment and be able to explain this clearly. It is good practice for the assessor to check that the student has received the report, understands it and knows what to do to move forwards, especially if the student's university does not provide this service.

Cautions when interpreting cognitive and attainment measures for HE students

Cognitive abilities

The pattern of scores should be noted, including any substantial difference between verbal and non-verbal ability as well as particular areas of strength. If a student's problems with aspects of expressive language appear to compromise their performance on the vocabulary scale, it is worth administering a test of receptive vocabulary.

When testing students whose first language is not English, the results of verbal measures must be interpreted with caution. It should not simply be assumed that verbal measures are lower because the student is using English as an additional language, but the test results might usefully be compared with the level of spoken language ability, and if considered appropriate, it could be noted in the report that the formal scores might under-represent the true verbal ability.

As in any diagnostic assessment, critical elements are measures of working memory, speed of processing and phonological abilities, the underlying cognitive processes.

At HE level, some students with an SpLD can perform reasonably well on measures of phonological awareness and the reasons for this need to be explored. It might be because the tests of phonological awareness are untimed, and the assessor may note that the student's skills in manipulating the sound structure of language are not the automatic ones expected and the formal score does not reflect or record the effort involved. The student may have received specialist teaching support in the past, which has trained his phonological awareness. He may have used visual strategies to 'see' the answers to the items. If the student has learned other languages he is likely to have gained additional training in the elementary skills of segmentation and blending of sounds. Sometimes additional testing, such as non-word phonological manipulations, may highlight underlying problems not apparent when real words are used.

It should be recognised that, at HE level, many students have compensated for some of their literacy difficulties and might perform adequately on tests of single-word reading and spelling accuracy. They do, however, encounter problems with more subtle and complex aspects of written language, and such difficulties are exacerbated when demands are made on their memory and organisational skills, as well as their ability to process information at speed.

Reading

At HE level, measures of reading will, at minimum, include single-word reading, timed word and non-word reading, an evaluation of continuous text reading, both oral and silent, reading speed and reading comprehension.

In a single-word reading task, note whether reading rate slows markedly as the student works through the test. How efficiently are letters mapped to sounds, and how easily can the student pronounce polysyllabic words? Note that when students have English as an additional language, it is unwise to record vowel misreadings as errors.

Sometimes it is only the timed measures of reading which reveal the inefficiencies in the mechanics of reading. Timed oral reading of continuous text can also reveal useful information about the student's reading fluency.

The standardised measure of silent reading comprehension will provide information about the student's ability to extract meaning from text. It might also be useful to include a measure of listening comprehension, particularly if the student's learning is likely to take place through listening to information.

Spelling

In a test of single-word spelling, note whether the student relies extensively on sound-letter translation and whether this is reliable; note also whether correctly spelled words are produced instantly, or are the result of several attempts. At HE level, many students will be able to produce reasonable phonetic approximations, but some may rely on a hazy recall of a word's visual appearance and as a result produce rather 'bizarre' spellings. The assessor might have to consider cases where a student no longer handwrites but types all notes and documents. If so, is spelling weaker because of the constant reliance on the computer spell-check, or perhaps because the kinaesthetic memory of the fingers on the keyboard is lost in handwriting?

Writing

A crucial test is a timed piece of free writing. This will provide information about the student's ability to manage language and organise a written response. The assessor, in discussion with the student, might establish an appropriate title, perhaps one similar to something he might be expected to tackle in his course of study, as this helps to set the task at the appropriate level.

The student's ability to communicate ideas, and to structure and organise these at sentence level and in the overall piece, should be noted, as well as his ability to spell in context, to use vocabulary effectively, and to retain grammatical and technical accuracy. Handwriting speed and legibility should also be recorded, and it is also very useful to review writing skills and speed when using a word processor, in order to inform decisions about examination arrangements.

Standardised tests of copying speed and pure handwriting speed also have a valuable place in the assessment. Results can be compared with the cognitive process of text composition described above. It should be noted that if a test uses a particular approach and title in the production of the norms, these norms can only be used if the test instructions are followed.

Numeracy and mathematics

At HE level, a test of numeracy or mathematics would not be included in a diagnostic assessment as a matter of course, but many degree courses do make demands on numeracy skills and these should be investigated if they are a cause for concern.

Recommendations and intervention at HE level

As always, the recommendations will use the information gathered on student's strengths and weaknesses to identify areas which will require support within the context of what is expected of the student on his degree course. The support might take a number of different forms, but the most common is the provision of specialist one-to-one teaching alongside items of specialist equipment and assistive software.

If the assessor feels that technological support, such as screen readers or voice-activated software, would be appropriate, then this should be made clear in the report. However, if the student is eligible to apply for DSA support, a DSA-funded 'Needs Assessment' will follow the diagnostic assessment and it is the Needs Assessor's role, in consultation with the student, to specify the particular programmes and hardware as well as the additional support the student needs.

Specialist study skills' training may be beneficial and the assessor is in a good position to indicate where the focus for the student should be placed. Possible areas include reading/research strategies, essay planning and writing skills, proof-reading, note-taking, learning technical or course-related spellings, word-finding strategies, spoken presentation skills, memory and revision strategies, examination techniques, organisational skills. Further ideas for supporting particular areas as appropriate will also be valuable.

Recommendations for assessment and examination adjustments should be made, if appropriate. It might be sufficient to recommend additional time for written examinations (25% is usual), but other adjustments may include the use of word processors, assistive software, readers, scribes, rest breaks, examination spacing or discretionary guidelines for the marking of assessed coursework. Flexible formats in coursework or examinations, the provision of questions on tape, vivas replacing or supporting written examinations and recorded submissions might be possible. However, assessors should be mindful that universities vary in their policies on examination arrangements. Some universities restrict the type of examination accommodations allowed, so it is helpful if the assessor is familiar with the procedures of the student's institution. It should be remembered we are advising on 'reasonable' adjustments and, while we are in a good position to provide specialist guidance, any recommendations which conflict with policy are best handled with caution and through liaison with the institution.

Other forms of institutional support, such as extended library loans, free photocopying, special small-group induction courses for the library or study skills workshops, may well be available, and the student needs to be reminded of these in the written report.

Referral to other professionals

It is helpful if the assessor is knowledgeable about the support (academic, counselling, mental health and well-being) and other accommodations available at the student's particular university and can give specific guidance as well as recommendations for onward referral, if appropriate, to other professionals in these services. The assessor must of course be aware of data protection issues, and check that the student has given permission for information disclosure before including sensitive information.

Dyspraxia

At HE level, the assessor will be able to make recommendations appropriate for the student with dyspraxia in the same way as for the student with dyslexia. For the 16+ age group, the specialist assessor can provide a label of dyspraxia, unlike younger age groups where confirmation is needed from a medical practitioner (see SASC guidance: www.sasc.org.uk).

ADHD

In a case where there are significant and pervasive difficulties with attention, clearly interfering with effort and performance, the assessor should summarise the nature of these and how they affect the student's study, in a similar way as for the student with other specific learning difficulties. Referral should also be made to specialist medical services, normally through the GP. However, appropriate recommendations which support the difficulties with attention will be made in the report (see Chapter 7) (see SASC guidance).

Visual stress

If a student reports visual disturbance when reading, it would be appropriate to screen for a visual stress condition or to recommend that the student's visual functioning is investigated further, for example by practitioners linked to the Institute of Optometry (www.ioo.org.uk). The assessment might need to be halted if difficulties appear to be substantial (see page 60).

Case study: Lucy

This thumbnail sketch of Lucy, age 20, provides an example of how an assessment might benefit a student in HE.

Standard Deviation	-3	-2	-1	0	+1	+2	+3
Standard Score	69–	70–84	85–89	90–110	111–115	116–130	131+
				Broad average range			
Tests: Cognitive Abilities							
Verbal ability						118	
Non-verbal ability				109			
Phonological awareness		80					
Phonological short-term memory				90			
Rapid automatic naming		77					
Visual processing speed (written)		73					
Verbal working memory		84					
Visual memory				94			
Tests: Literacy Skills							
Reading accuracy – single word				104			
Sight-word reading (timed)			89				
Non-word reading (timed)		78					
Reading comprehension (untimed)				103			
Spelling – single word			86				
Copying speed				94			
Non-standardised tests							
Reading speed: aloud	120 words per minute – below expectation						
Reading speed: silent	160 words per minute – below expectation						
Free writing speed: handwriting	17 words per minute – below expectation						
Free writing speed: word processing	22 words per minute – below expectation						

This layout is limited to standard scores only for the purposes of presenting a brief case study; assessors will wish to adapt their own score presentation style to include further test and technical detail (see Chapter 8).

Lucy was referred because since working at degree level, she has struggled with literacy tasks and she has noticed that she takes much longer than other students to complete assignments. She also has problems with note-taking and with examinations. She is in her second year of a BSc in Social Policy with Social Psychology.

Test results revealed underlying weaknesses in phonological processing, working memory and processing speed, but above-average verbal ability, average non-verbal ability and average single-word reading and spelling skills. Her difficulties affect many study activities, but very notably her ability to write in a fluent and ordered way. Lucy has a profile of dyslexia.

Main recommendations were as follows:

- Lucy would benefit from specialist teaching in study skills, particularly in the organisation of writing, in memory and revision techniques, as well as general organisational skills across a range of activities.
- She would find extended library loans helpful.
- She should make an application for DSA support on her university course. A text-to-speech program and a way of supporting note-taking in lectures would be particularly beneficial.
- Lucy should request the following adjustments in examinations:
  - additional time (25%) to complete written papers;
  - the use of a word processor to type her examination scripts (her handwriting rapidly deteriorates after a short period of time).

Summary

This is an exciting and constructive time in HE, with institutions working to establish a solid culture of awareness and a framework of support. However, assessment at this level is no easy task, and assessors need to be conversant with the demands of HE, and with the subtleties and complexities of the issues involved. The life experiences the adult brings to the task, as well as the coping strategies they have developed over the years, combine to make their profile a rich and complex one. As assessors, we have to interpret the whole picture and create a positive way forward.

PART FOUR

Resources and Reference

Miscue analysis

Miscue analysis is a technique to assess strategies used to read continuous prose. It can be carried out as part of a reading test or with any suitably demanding continuous text. Since about twenty errors are needed for the analysis, a good estimation of the individual's reading skills is needed first in order to choose suitable material.

- If not using a standardised test record form, photocopy the chosen text to use as a record sheet.
- Note how the individual attempts to read all the words with which he has difficulty. Do not just put ticks and crosses. You may choose to make a recording so you can listen again.

There are two stages in the analysis:

1. Catalogue all the errors into categories as follows and consider the balance of error-types: **Substitutions** (words read incorrectly, as other real words or as non-words), **self-corrections**, **refusals, insertions** and **omissions**.

Note: self-corrections are a good sign, as they show that sentence structure and meaning are being used to inform a further successful attempt. If *'said'* is not recognised, but sounded out as *'s–a–i–d'* and then read correctly when its meaning has become clear, the reader is clearly beginning to use 'top-down' strategies.

2. Then, carry out the next level of analysis on just the **substitutions**. Draw up a table to show which cueing systems the reader has used for each one. Did he respond with a word that looked similar to the target (grapho-phonic cue)? Was his response appropriate for the sentence structure (syntactic cue)? Did his response make sense within the passage, showing he is making use of semantic cues and trying to read for meaning?

Target and response	Grapho-phonic?	Syntactic?	Semantic?
certain 'curtain'	Yes	No	No
daring 'darling'	Yes	No	No
huge 'large'	Perhaps (–ge)	Yes	Yes
concealed 'hidden'	No	yes	Yes

Add up the number of positives in each column, and compare the totals. It becomes clear if the individual is, for example, relying heavily on the grapho-phonic cueing system, but not thinking about syntax, or making a real effort to gain or preserve meaning. 'Yes' in two (or all three) columns, for the same word, would indicate that the reader is simultaneously processing at different levels – word and/or sentence and/or text.

This type of analysis will support decisions and justify advice about how to help the weak reader develop more effective strategies, and can be included in the commentary in the diagnostic report.

Screening: an alternative

What follows is a suggested format for group screening the literacy skills of older pupils and college students in a way that will support those who are weaker and not patronise their more academic peers (an equally valid consideration). The basic procedure could also be used by diagnostic assessors to explore individual skills and strategies prior to, or as part of, a full diagnostic process.

This approach yields valuable data for mainstream and specialist staff alike. Students are screened in small groups of up to fifteen by subject, with instructions or questions carefully composed at a level to suit them; the process takes up to two hours. It can be closely tailored to students' interests and asks students to consider independently their learning strengths and styles. Professionals with experience of students with SpLDs will be able to spot characteristic traits in the material produced.

Note-taking: 5-minute independent note-taking task

This is a good place to start, as most students will recognise this is a necessary skill for study. Students are asked to take notes on an introductory talk of no more than 5 minutes, which is given without visual aids or handouts. At the end, students are asked to evaluate if they could make sense of their notes in six months' time – stress that it is only important they understand them; extend the task by asking them to write down if they find note-taking easy or difficult, or if they use alternate strategies.

Reading: 10-minute subject-related cloze exercise

To gain a view of reading accuracy, comprehension and speed, a timed cloze exercise is useful. A short, course-related passage of around 200 words is prepared with the first sentence intact, but approximately every sixth subsequent word deleted, ensuring that a mixture of word types are omitted. Test out the piece with colleagues or existing students (with average reading skills) and record the time taken. It should be completed comfortably in around 10 minutes. Allow this amount of time for the screening task.

At the end, again ask students to evaluate their performance. Those who found it easy will be reassured, those who could not complete the task but were accurate will need to allow extra time for reading, and those who finished but who could not supply the missing words will likely have the greatest need. Both latter groups might need further assessment for examination access arrangements.

Spelling and punctuation – 50-word subject-related passage dictation

Standardised spelling tests assess if skills are age-appropriate, but the words are not necessarily those needed for students' courses. They will probably get by in life without ever knowing how many *c*'s and *s*'s there are in *necessary*, but it is important that a student of Travel and Tourism can spell *tourism*, for example. This should never be taken for granted.

To assess course-related skills, select a short passage from a course text, or create a new passage, which includes relevant vocabulary – students will accept these are words they need to spell correctly. Read it through once to the group and then dictate in small chunks and at a pace to accommodate the slowest writer. Then read through again at normal speed, clearly using punctuation. Lists can be included in the passage to check use of commas.

All students are asked to note how well they thought they did, any strategies they use for spelling or indeed if they would like help. The beauty of this method is everything is dealt with in confidence and everyone writes something at the end, not just those who found it difficult.

Summarising: a combined reading comprehension and writing composition task

This is an area where many students experience difficulty, as it is a rarely practised skill. A not too lengthy course-related article with a clear underlying message should be selected, and the assessor should check she is able to summarise it in three or four sentences within 10 to 15 minutes. This is the task that is set for the students.

Again, students reflect on their skills. Some will highlight sections of the text and simply copy them, others will use their own words but write almost as much as the original, others will know what to do but run out of time. All these students might agree they have not 'fully mastered' the skills needed (note they do not need to admit they 'do not know how' to summarise) and will need some guidance to be successful independent learners.

Mind-mapping

Some students will have found the screening thus far quite taxing; the following exercise should help release some tension. The assessor decides on a suitably provocative topic and explains the concept of mind-mapping; most students are familiar with it, but might know it by a different name. The assessor acts as scribe and tries to create order out of the mayhem that ensues when she invites comment. There will be dominant group members; others will say nothing. This is their choice. Fifteen minutes should be allowed at most for this activity.

On this occasion, students should reflect on whether they preferred this group work to the individual tasks. Those who did might consider study groups for assignment planning. Those who did not wish to contribute could think how they might develop confidence for public speaking, as it will often be part of course tasks.

And finally... evaluation of preferred learning styles

Reflecting on a study subject they enjoy, students are asked to think what it was that made the learning easy and the teaching memorable. Explicit acknowledgement of successful teaching and learning strategies is a positive way to close, and ideas may be shared and used to go forward.

Review

Everything that has been produced is handed in, reviewed and used to inform the first individual tutorial between course tutor and student. The review is undoubtedly a time-consuming process, but it can be a clear basis for study skills teaching and is an informal, non-threatening way to identify those who might have a specific difficulty.

Key features of a teaching programme

Long-terms aims should be identified first. These will link with the overall curriculum, vocational or examination goals, as appropriate.

The next task is to set **short-term targets**. The writing of specific, measurable, achievable, relevant and time-related (SMART) targets for each of the areas to be addressed will help the learner and his teacher know where they are going. For example, *'James should aim to develop his confidence in spelling'* helps no-one – we doubtless knew that already – but *'James will be able to spell* said*, because, they, and* have *at word and sentence level with 95% accuracy in week 6'* is clear. Setting out with high expectations but identifying achievable goals for the programme within the time available will ensure the learner feels and sees his developing success; too many goals are dispiriting, too few are insufficiently challenging. The targets should be something which the learner needs and wants to learn. The pace of the teaching is also an important aspect. The programme should indicate when targets are introduced and how frequently they are to be revisited and assessed.

Each short-term target should have an explanation of the **methods** by which it will be achieved – built on firm multisensory teaching principles. The methods should be clear enough to enable the person delivering the programme to work effectively with the learner without the need for further explanation or research. They should take account of the individual learner's interests wherever possible to promote enjoyment in learning – a little fun goes a long way.

Also note the **resources** required, with sources noted for any specialist tools not readily available in schools and references for any published resources recommended – although these should never take the place of individualised targets. A recommendation to work through pages 3–8 of a scheme does not usually provide the impetus for exciting teaching.

Of course, the point at which the programme is to be **reviewed** and new targets devised will also be clear. It is important to evaluate the effectiveness of the programme in terms of both targets and methods to ensure efficient use of time and resources is being made for the best advantage of the learner.

Test information

Please note: the following list is comprehensive but it is not exhaustive. Many of the tests in common current use are listed here, but assessors must regularly re-evaluate their test resources to ensure they continue to represent the most up-to-date available normative data.

Cognitive Abilities: Underlying Ability

Name of Test / Where and when published	Age Range	Use*	Notes
British Picture Vocabulary Test – 3rd edition (BPVS III) UK / 2009	3–16	I	Receptive language Supplementary norms for pupils with English as an additional language (EAL)
Expressive Vocabulary Test – 2nd edition (EVT-2) USA / 2007	2:6–90	I	Expressive language If used with PPVT–4 (below), can directly compare levels of receptive and expressive vocabulary
Kaufman Brief Intelligence Test – 2nd edition (K-BIT) USA / 2004	4–90	I	Receptive and expressive language, nonverbal reasoning
Naglieri Nonverbal Ability Test USA / 2003	5–17	I / G	Nonverbal reasoning
Peabody Picture Vocabulary Test – 4th edition (PPVT-4) USA / 2007	2:6–90+	I	Receptive language
Ravens Progressive Matrices and Vocabulary Scales UK Norms / 2008	7–18	I / G	Vocabulary and nonverbal reasoning
Wide Range Intelligence Test (WRIT) USA / 2000	4–84	I	Verbal ability (vocabulary knowledge and verbal reasoning – receptive and expressive language) Nonverbal ability (2 subtests)

*Use: I denotes *individual*; G denotes *group* test administration

Cognitive Ability: Phonological Abilities

Name of Test / Where and when published	Age Range	Use*	Notes
Comprehensive Test of Phonological Processing – 2nd edition (CTOPP-2) USA / 2013	5–24:11	I	Phonological awareness, phonological memory, phonological processing speed (rapid naming)
Dyslexia Portfolio UK / 2008	6–15:11	I	Phonological skills, rapid-naming skills, working memory (also tests some reading and writing skills)
Perin's Spoonerism Task UK / 1983	14–25	I	Now very old – could be used qualitatively. Phonological awareness + working memory
Phonological Assessment Battery (PhAB) UK / 1997	6–14:11	I	Phonological awareness, phonological and semantic fluency, phonemic decoding, phonological processing speed. Some timed subtests allow analysis of automaticity and speed of processing
Woodcock-Reading Mastery Tests – 3rd edition (WRMT-III) USA / 2011	4.6– 8.11	I	First and last sound matching, Rhyme production, Blending deletion Object and colour naming Number and letter naming, plus a comprehensive battery of reading tests

Cognitive Abilities: Visual Processing Speed

Name of Test / Where and when published	Age Range	Use*	Notes
Symbol Digit Modalities Test (SDMT) USA / 1982	8–Adult	I / G	Visual processing speed and visual-motor skills. Written (group/individual), Oral (individual)
Wordchains UK / 1999	7–18	I / G	Visual tracking skills / reading efficiency

Cognitive Abilities: Short-term and Working Memory

Name of Test / Where and when published	Age Range	Use*	Notes
Automated Working Memory Assessment – 2nd edition (AWMA-2) UK / 2012	5–79	I / G	Working memory (visual and verbal) Screener, Short form and long form. On-line assessment. Annual licence
Comprehensive Test of Phonological Processing – 2nd edition (CTOPP–2) USA / 2013	5–24:11	I	Short-term forward memory (but no measure of working memory)
Dyslexia Portfolio UK / 2008	6–15:11	I	Contains a working memory subtest. Also rapid-naming skills, phonological skills, with reading and writing
NAB Digits Forward/Digits Backward Test USA / 2003	18–97	I	Norms for forwards and reverse. Part of the NAB Attention Module, but available separately
Test of Memory and Learning 2 (TOMAL 2) USA / 2007	5–59.11	I	Verbal and visual short-term and working memory Comprehensive battery of subtests
Wide Range Assessment of Memory and Learning – 2nd edition (WRAML-2) USA / 2003	5–90	I	Verbal and visual short-term and working memory Comprehensive battery of subtests

Visual / Motor Integration Abilities

Name of Test / Where and when published	Age Range	Use*	Notes
Beery-Buktenica Developmental Test of Visual-Motor Integration – 6th edition (BEERY VMI) USA / 2010	2–100	I / G	Visual motor integration, visual perception, visual-motor skills
Full Range Test of Visual Motor Integration (FRTVMI) USA / 2005	5–74	I / G	Visual-motor skills. Revision of the TVMI
Morrisby Manual Dexterity Test UK / 2003	14–Adult	I / G	Visual-motor skills and manual dexterity. *This test has been withdrawn from approved test list for Disabled Student's Allowance applications*
Test of Visual Motor Skills – 3rd edition (TVMS-3) USA / 2009	3–90	I / G	Visual-motor skills
Test of Visual-Perceptual Skills (non-motor) – 3rd edition (TVPS-3) USA / 2006	4–18.11	I / G	Visual-perceptual skills: the ability to make sense out of what is seen.
Symbol Digit Modalities Test (SDMT) USA / 1982	8–Adult	I / G	Speed of processing plus some elements of visual motor skills. Written and oral versions
Wide Range Assessment of Visual Motor Ability (WRAVMA) USA / 1995	3–17	I	Visual-spatial, fine motor, and integrated visual-motor skills

Single-word Reading

Name of Test / Where and when published	Age Range	Use*	Notes
Dyslexia Portfolio UK / 2008	6–15:11	I	Also tests some writing and cognitive processing skills
Hodder Group Reading Tests 1–3 – 2nd edition (HGRT) UK / 2007	5–16+	I / G	Word, sentence and text-level reading comprehension
Hodder Oral Reading Tests (HORT) UK / 2006	5–16:09	I	Single-word reading, sentence reading and reading speed
Single Word Reading Test (SWRT) UK / 2007	6–16	I	Oral single-word reading
Wechsler Individual Achievement Test – 2nd UK edition for Teachers (WIAT-II-UK-T) UK / 2006	4–85:11 UK norms: 4–16.11 US norms: 17–85	I	Single-word reading accuracy, text-level reading comprehension and reading speed (also tests spelling) Reading speed: 6–16.11 Words per minute (WPM) – for KS4 access arrangements
Wide Range Achievement Test – 4th edition (WRAT-4) USA / 2006	5–94	I	Single-word reading accuracy and sentence-level reading comprehension (also tests spelling, arithmetic)
Woodcock-Reading Mastery Tests – 3rd edition (WRMT-III) USA / 2011	6–Adult	I	Comprehensive battery of reading tests

Non-word Reading

Name of Test / Where and when published	Age Range	Use*	Notes
Nonword Reading Test (NWRT) UK / 2004	6–16	I	Timed phonemic decoding. Two parallel forms
Test of Word Reading Efficiency – 2nd edition (TOWRE -2) USA / 2011	6–24:11	I	Timed non-word reading and timed sight-word reading test. Four equivalent forms.

Reading Comprehension

Name of Test / Where and when published	Age Range	Use*	Notes
Access Reading Test UK / 2006	7–20+	I / G	Silent sentence and text-level test. Parallel forms
Adult Reading Test (ART) UK / 2004	16–25+	I	Oral, text-level test. Also includes accuracy and rate measures
Advanced Reading Comprehension Test (ARC) UK / 2001	18+	I	Silent reading comprehension. Normed on first year university students. Two forms
Diagnostic Reading Analysis – 2nd edition (DRA) UK / 2008	7–16:05	I	Reading accuracy, comprehension, and fluency/reading rate. Designed for less able readers and incorporates a passage for assessing listening comprehension: this determines the start point for reading assessment. Two parallel forms. Also Diagnostic Profiler CD-ROM
Edinburgh Reading Test 4 (ERT4) UK / 2002	11–16	I / G	Silent sentence and text-level under timed conditions. Reading: skimming, understanding vocabulary, reading for facts and opinions, and inferential comprehension.
Edinburgh Reading Test 4–Interactive (ERT4i) UK / 2002	11:7–Adult	I	Silent sentence and text level
Gray Oral Reading Tests – 5th edition (GORT 5) 2012 / USA	6–23:11	I	Measures of rate, accuracy, fluency, and comprehension. Parallel forms.
Gray Silent Reading Test (GSRT) USA / 2002	7–25	I / G	Silent text-level reading comprehension
Group Reading Scales UK / 2009	5–13:3 9–16+	G	Reading comprehension via multiple-choice sentence-completion questions With Scorer/Profiler CD Rom for analysing results. Two parallel forms
Hodder Group Reading Tests 1–3 – 2nd edition (HGRT) UK / 2007	5–9 7–12 9.5–16+5 –	I / G	Word, sentence and text-level reading comprehension. Two parallel forms of each test. With Scorer/Profiler CD-ROM
Hodder Oral Reading Tests (HORT) UK / 2006	5–16:09	I	Single-word reading, sentence reading and reading speed
Neale Analysis of Reading Ability – 2nd edition (NARA 2) UK / 1997	6–12. 11	I	Accuracy, speed and comprehension. Two forms

Name of Test / Where and when published	Age Range	Use*	Notes
NFER Reading Assessment for Years 3, 4 and 5 NFER UK / 2012	Key Stage 2	G	Reading booklets for each year group contain a variety of text types, fiction and non-fiction, with a mixture of question types including multiple choice, sequencing and thought bubbles.
New Group Reading Test – 3rd edition (NGRT -3) UK / 2010	6–16	G	Sentence completion and passage comprehension at all levels. At higher levels includes range of skills contributing to reading comprehension
New Salford Sentence Reading Test UK / 2013	5:6–11:3	I	Oral reading based on sentences of graded difficulty. Provides reading accuracy plus optional measure of reading comprehension For less able readers: up to 13 For comprehension: up to 14 Three parallel forms
Suffolk Reading Scale 2 (SRS–2) UK (2002) **SRS Digital** UK (2008)	6–14.11 SRS Digital: 17.4	I / G	Multiple-choice and sentence-completion questions. Paper and digital (on-line) formats. *3 comparable levels SRS Digital includes* Level 4 for 14-16 year-olds, a screener for access arrangements
Wechsler Individual Achievement Test – 2nd UK edition for Teachers (WIAT-II-UK-T) UK / 2006	4–85:11	I	Text-level reading comprehension and reading speed (also tests single-word reading and spelling accuracy)
Wide Range Achievement Test – 4th edition (WRAT- 4) USA / 2006	5–94	I	Sentence-level reading comprehension (also tests single-word reading, spelling, arithmetic)
Wide Range Achievement Test – Expanded (WRAT-E) Group Form USA / 2001	7–18:11	G	Silent reading comprehension – text-level (also tests maths; nonverbal reasoning)
Wide Range Achievement Test – Expanded (WRAT-E) Individual Form USA / 2001	5–24:11	I	Reading comprehension – text-level (also tests maths, nonverbal reasoning)

Name of Test / Where and when published	Age Range	Use*	Notes
York Assessment of Reading for Comprehension (YARK) UK / 2010	Early Reading: 4–7 Passage Reading 5–11 Passage Reading Secondary 11–16	I	*Early Reading*: letter-sound knowledge, early word recognition, sound isolation, sound deletion *Passage Reading:* – Reading fluency, accuracy and reading comprehension *Passage Reading Secondary,* fiction and non-fiction prose passages. Reading rate, reading accuracy, (supplementary passages only), reading comprehension, reading fluency, single-word reading. Also passages for students with reading age below age 10, accessible at a reading age of 6:5.
Woodcock-Reading Mastery Tests: 3rd edition (WRMT-III) USA / 2011	6–Adult	I	Comprehensive battery of reading tests

Listening Comprehension

Name of Test / Where and when published	Age Range	Use*	Notes
Oral and Written Language Scales – 2nd edition (OWLS-II™ LC/OE and RC/WE) USA / 2011	3–21.11	I	Listening comprehension and oral expression scales Reading comprehension and written expression scales. Lexical/semantics, syntax, pragmatics, supralinguistics
Woodcock-Reading Mastery Tests – 3rd edition (WRMT-III) USA / 2011	6–Adult	I	Comprehensive battery of reading tests

Single-word Spelling

Name of Test / Where and when published	Age Range	Use*	Notes
British Spelling Test Series – 2nd edition UK / 2009	6–13	I / G	Assesses spelling at word, sentence and continuous writing level
Diagnostic Spelling Tests 1–5 UK / 2006	9–25+	I / G	Two parallel forms of each test
Dyslexia Portfolio UK / 2008	6–15:11	I	Also tests some reading and cognitive processing skills
Helen Arkell Spelling Test - 2nd edition (HAST 2) UK / 2013	5–17+	I	Re-standardised on large sample group. The words represent the normal development of spelling. Diagnostic test which supports categorisation of errors. Now two parallel forms
Single Word Spelling Test (SWST) UK / 2001	6–14	I / G	A set of nine tests each containing between 30 and 50 words
Wechsler Individual Achievement Test – 2nd UK edition for Teachers (WIAT-II-UK-T) UK / 2006	4–85:11	I	Also tests single-word reading, comprehension
Wide Range Achievement Test – 4th edition (WRAT-4) USA / 2006	5–94	I / G	Also tests single-word reading, sentence comprehension
Vernon Graded Word Spelling Test – 3rd edition UK / 2006	5–18+	I / G	Revised and re-standardised

Handwriting Skills

Name of Test / Where and when published	Age Range	Use*	Skill
Detailed Assessment of Speed of Handwriting (DASH) UK / 2007	9–16:11	I / G	Free writing speed, copying speed (best and fast), graphic speed, alphabet writing speed plus qualitative evaluation of writing
Detailed Assessment of Speed of Handwriting (DASH 17+) UK / 2010	17–25	I / G	As above
Free writing	All		See Chapters 5 and 6
Please note the following tests have deliberately been **excluded** as their norms are now outdated and alternatives are available: **Hedderley Sentence Completion Test** and **Allcock Handwriting Assessment**. Assessors might on occasion use them for qualitative investigation.			

Tests of Language

Name of Test / Where and when published	Age Range	Use*	Notes
Test of Written Language – 4th edition (TOWL-4) USA / 2008	9–17:11	I	Vocabulary, spelling, punctuation, logical sentences, sentence combining, contextual conventions, story composition
Test of Adolescent and Adult Language – 4th edition (TOAL-4) USA / 2007	12–24:11	I / G	Word opposites, word derivations, spoken analogies, word similarities, sentence combining, orthographic usage
Test of Language Development – 4th edition (TOLD-P:4) USA / 2008	4–8.11 / 8–17	I	*Primary Edition:* nine subtests measure different components of spoken language. *Intermediate Edition:* six subtests that measure semantics (i.e. meaning and thought) or grammar (i.e. syntax and morphology) skills
Test For Reception of Grammar – 2nd edition (TROG-2) UK / 2003	4–16.11	I	Grammatical comprehension. Also adult sample

Numeracy and Mathematics

Name of Test / Where and when published	Age Range	Use*	Notes
Access Mathematics Tests UK / 2008	7–12 / 11–16+	I / G	Two tests (for primary and secondary/FE) each with two parallel forms. Pencil and paper version
Access Mathematics Tests – Interactive UK / 2008	7–16+	I	On-screen standardised assessment with instant, automated marking and reporting. Single-user and networkable CD-ROMs
Basic Number Diagnostic Test – 3rd edition UK / 2001	5–7	I	Diagnosis and follow-up in basic number skills. Comprehensive battery covering twelve different skills
Mathematics Competency Test UK / 2002	11:6–18	I / G	Can provide useful information about how literacy and language skills affect maths learning
NFER Mathematics assessment for Years 3, 4 and 5 UK / 2012	Key Stage 2	G	A mix of different types of question
Wide Range Achievement Test – Expanded (WRAT-E) Individual Form USA / 2001	5–24:11	I	Mathematical understanding and reasoning (with an emphasis on problem solving). Also Reading comprehension – text-level nonverbal reasoning

Test References

Access Reading Test, 2006, McCarty, C. and Crumpler, M.: Hodder Education

Access Mathematics Tests, 2008, McCarty, C.: Hodder Education

Adult Reading Test, 2004, Brooks, P., Everatt, J. and Fidler, R.: Roehampton University

Advanced Reading Comprehension Test (ARC), 2001, Singleton, C. and Simmons, F.: University of Hull

Basic Number Diagnostic Test, 3rd edition, 2001, Gillham, B.: Hodder and Stoughton

Automated Working Memory Assessment, 2nd edition (AWMA–2), 2012, Packiam-Alloway, T.: Pearson Assessment

Beery Buktenica Developmental Test of Visual-Motor Integration, 6th edition (BEERY VMI), 2010, Beery, K. E., Buktenica, N. A. and Beery, .N. A.: Pearson Assessment

British Picture Vocabulary Test, 3rd edition (BPVS III), 2009, Dunn, L. M. and Dunn, D. M.: NFER Nelson

British Spelling Test Series, 2nd edition, 2009, Vincent, D. and de la Mare, M.: London, GL Assessment

Comprehensive Test of Phonological Processing, 2nd edition (CTOPP – 2), 2013, Wagner, R., Torgeson, J. K. and Rashotte, C. A. and Pearson, N.A.: Pro-Ed

Detailed Assessment of Handwriting Speed (DASH), 2007, Barnett, A., Henderson, S., Scheib, B. and Schulz, J.: Pearson Assessment

Detailed Assessment of Speed of Handwriting (DASH 17+), 2010, Barnett, A., Henderson, S., Scheib, B. and Schulz, J.: Pearson Assessment

Diagnostic Reading Analysis, 2nd edition (DRA), 2008, Crumpler, M. and McCarty, C.: Hodder Education

Diagnostic Spelling Tests, 2006, Crumpler M. and McCarty, C.: Hodder Education

Dyslexia Portfolio, 2008, Turner, M.: G L Assessment

Edinburgh Reading Test 4 (ERT4), 2002, University of Edinburgh: Hodder Education

Edinburgh Reading Test 4 – Interactive (ERT4i), 2002, University of Edinburgh: Hodder Education

Expressive Vocabulary Test, 2nd edition (EVT-2), 2007, Williams, K.: Pearson Assessment

Full Range Test of Visual Motor Integration (FRTVMI), 2005, Hammill, D., Pearson, N., Voress, J. and Reynolds, C.: Pro-Ed

Gray Oral Reading Tests, 5th edition (GORT-5), 2012, Wiederholt, J. L. and Bryant, R.: Pro-Ed

Gray Silent Reading Test (GSRT), 2000, Wiederholt, J. L. and Blalock, G.: Pro-Ed

Group Reading Scales, 2009, Vincent, D. and Crumpler, M.: Hodder Education

Helen Arkell Spelling Test, 2nd edition (HAST 2), 2013, Caplan, M., Banc, C. and McLean, B.: Helen Arkell Dyslexia Centre

Hodder Group Reading Tests, 2nd edition (HGRT), 2007, Vincent, D. and Crumpler, M.: Hodder Education

Hodder Oral Reading Tests (HORT), 2006, Vincent, D. and Crumpler, M.: Hodder Education

Kaufman Brief Intelligence Test, 2nd edition (K-BIT), 2004, Kaufman, A. S. and Kaufman, N. L.: Pearson Assessment

Mathematics Competency Test, 2002, Vernon, P. E., Miller, K M and Izard, J F: Hodder Education

NAB Digits Forward/Digits Backward Test, 2003, Stern, R. A. and White, T.: Psychological Assessment Resources

Naglieri Nonverbal Ability Test (NNAT), 2003, Naglieri, J. A.: Pearson Assessment

Neale Analysis of Reading Ability: Second Revised British edition (NARA 2), 1997, Neale, M.: NFER-Nelson

New Group Reading Test (NGRT), 3rd edition, 2010, Burge, B., Styles, B., Brzyska, B., Cooper, L., Shamsan, Y., Saltini, F. and Twist, L: GL Assessment and the National Foundation for Educational Research (NFER)

NFER Reading Assessment for Years 3, 4 and 5, 2012: NFER

NFER Mathematics Assessment for Years 3, 4, and 5, 2012: NFER

New Salford Sentence Reading Test, 2013, G. E. Bookbinder; revised and restandardised by McCarty, C. and Lallaway, M.: Hodder Education

Nonword Reading Test (NWRT), 2004, Crumpler, M. and McCarty, C.: Hodder Education

Oral and Written Language Scales, Second edition (OWLS-II™ LC/OE and RC/WEm), 2011, Carrow-Woolfolk, E.: Pearson Education

Peabody Picture Vocabulary Test, 4th edition (PPVT- 4), 2007, Dunn, L. M. and Dunn, D. M.: Pearson Assessment

Perin's Spoonerism Test, 1983, Perin, D.: available from Dyslexia Action website

Phonological Assessment Battery (PhAB), 1997, Fredrickson, N., Frith, U. and Reason, R.: NFER Nelson

Ravens Progressive Matrices & Vocabulary Scales, 2008, Raven, J. C., Court, J. H. and Raven, J.: Pearson Assessment

Single Word Reading Test (SWRT), 2007, Foster, H.: GL Assessment

Single Word Spelling Test (SWST), 2001, Sacre, L. and Masterton, J.: GL Assessment

Single Word Spelling Test Digital (SWST Digital), 2008, GL Assessment

Suffolk Reading Scale 2 (SRS – 2), 2002, Hagley, F.: GL Assessment

Suffolk Reading Scale Digital (SRS Digital), 2008, Hagley, F.: GL Assessment

Symbol Digit Modalities Test (SDMT), 1982, Smith, A.: Western Psychological Services

Test for Reception of Grammar, 2nd edition (TROG-2), 2003, Bishop, D.: Pearson Assessment

Test of Adolescent and Adult Language, 4th edition (TOAL-4), 2007, Hammill, D., Brown, V. L., Stephen, C., Larsen, S. C. and Wiederholt, J. L.: Pro-Ed

Test of Language Development-Primary, Fourth edition (TOLD-P:4) 2008, Hammill, D. and Newcomer, P. L.: Pro-Ed

Test of Memory and Learning 2 (TOMAL 2), 2007, Reynolds, C. R. and Bigler, E. D.: Pro-Ed

Test of Visual Motor Skills, 3rd edition (TVMS-3), 2009, Martin, N.: Psychological and Educational Publications Inc

Test of Visual-Perceptual Skills (non-motor), 3rd edition (TVPS-3) (2006), Martin, N.: Academic Therapy Publications

Test of Word Reading Efficiency 2 (TOWRE 2), 2011, Torgesen, J. K., Wagner, R. and Rashotte, C: Pro-Ed

Test of Written Language, 4th edition (TOWL-4), 2008, Hammill, D. and Larsen, S.: Pro-Ed

The Morrisby Manual Dexterity Test, part of Morrisby Profile 1991(revised), 2003, Morrisby, J. R., Morrisby, M. J. and Fox, G. D.: The Morrisby Organisation

Vernon Graded Word Spelling Test, 3rd edition, 2006, Vernon, P. E.: Revised by Crumpler, M. and McCarty, C.: Hodder Education

Wechsler Individual Achievement Test, 2nd UK edition For Teachers (WIAT-II-UK-T), 2006, Wechsler, D.: Pearson Assessment

Wide Range Achievement Test, 4th edition (WRAT4), 2006, Wilkinson, G. S. and Robertson, G. J.: Psychological Assessment Resources Inc

Wide Range Achievement Test – Expanded (WRAT-E), 2001, Wilkinson, G. S. and Robertson, G. J.: Psychological Assessment Resources Inc

Wide Range Assessment of Memory and Learning, 2nd edition (WRAML-2), 2003, Sheslow, D. and Adams, W.: Psychological Assessment Resources Inc

Wide Range Intelligence Test (WRIT), 2000, Glutting, J., Adams, W. and Sheslow, D.: Psychological Assessment Resources Inc

Wide Range Assessment of Visual Motor Ability (WRAVMA), 1995, Adams, W. and Sheslow, D.: Psychological Assessment Resources Inc

Woodcock-Reading Mastery Tests, 3rd edition (WRMT-III), 2011, Woodcock, R. W.: Pearson Assessment

Wordchains, 1999, Guron, L. M.: NFER Nelson

Working Memory Test Battery for Children (WMTB-C), 2001, Pickering, S. and Gathercole, S.: Pearson Assessment

York Assessment of Reading for Comprehension (YARC), 2010, Snowling, M. J., Stothard, S. E., Clance, P., Bowyer-Crane, C. D., Harrington, A., Truelove, E. and Hulme, C.: GL Assessment

Some source contact websites:

Ann Arbor	www.annarbor.co.uk
Dyslexia Action	www.dyslexiaaction.org.uk
GL Assessment (previously NFER-Nelson)	www.gl-assessment.co.uk
Helen Arkell Dyslexia Centre	www.arkellcentre.org.uk
Hodder Education	www.hoddereducation.co.uk / www.hoddertests.co.uk
Hogrefe Limited	www.hogrefe.co.uk
NFER	www.nfer.ac.uk
Patoss	www.patoss-dyslexia.org
Pearson	www.psychcorp.co.uk